THE
COVENTRY
CITY
MISCELLANY

THE
COVENTRY
CITY
MISCELLANY

MICHAEL KEANE

The
History
Press

First published 2011

The History Press
The Mill, Brimscombe Port
Stroud, Gloucestershire, GL5 2QG
www.thehistorypress.co.uk

British Library Cataloguing in Publication Data.
A catalogue record for this book is available from the British Library.

ISBN 978 0 7524 6075 8

Typesetting and origination by The History Press
Printed in Great Britain
Manufacturing managed by Jellyfish Print Solutions Ltd

ACKNOWLEDGEMENTS

Thanks are due to several people who have helped me put this book together. From years ago, thanks to Paul Wheeler and Neville Hadsley, who encouraged my scribbling in their Coventry City fanzines, *In Dublin's Fair City* and *Gary Mabbutt's Knee*. Thanks also to my very patient editor, Michelle Tilling, of The History Press. A large thank you to the players of Coventry City over the four decades I have been watching them, for providing much entertainment and many happy memories. Finally, my biggest thanks of all is to my own team at home, my wife Gabby and our own back four: Thomas, Oliver, Patrick and Annabelle.

Michael Keane, 2011

KICKING OFF

The Coventry City Football Club that we know today has its origins far, far away from the modern purpose-built stadium that is the Ricoh Arena. Way back in 1883 there were no handy motorway links, no attached retail parks and no underground casinos. What there was though was just as important as any of the modern-day criteria for a new stadium – there was the interest and enthusiasm of a group of people who loved their football.

Led by employee Willie Stanley, a group of workers from the Singer cycle factory met in the Aylesford Inn in Hillfields and it was there that a new football team was formed – Singers FC. In the latter part of the nineteenth century football was taking off; factory workers up and down the country had started to enjoy the new, cheap entertainment that organised football provided. New teams, new stadiums and new loyalties emerged up and down the country and Coventry was no different.

Singers FC tapped into that growing enthusiasm and within ten years of forming they won the prestigious Birmingham Junior Cup in consecutive years – 1891 and 1892. By 1899, the fledgling factory team would become Coventry City Football Club and new chapters were waiting to be written.

HOME FROM HOME

In the 112 years since Singers FC became Coventry City, two home grounds have been used for all but one of those seasons – Highfield Road and the Ricoh Arena. In their first ever season, 1898/99, City called their Stoke Road ground, just off Paynes Lane, home; but it was only a matter of a long goal-kick from the Highfield Road site where they were to stay for more than a century.

The Highfield Road era spanned three centuries, two world wars (one of which damaged the stadium) and oversaw enormous changes – from the first days of the professional game, through to the times of the hard-working, but low-paid players, into the modern era of the generously rewarded, well-drilled teams of athletes. In their 106-year stay, City had played their own version of the Football League's snakes and ladders, first rising in their early days, then falling back; before spectacularly rising to the very summit and enjoying the view for 34 years, only to slip down once more. Many times, it seemed as though those twin imposters of triumph and defeat might have been season-ticket holders!

When the plans for the move to the Ricoh were first announced, it was like watching *Tomorrow's World* all over again, as the purpose-built stadium of the future, with its retractable roof and sliding pitch, was unveiled. The plans were downgraded a little, but what was left was still an ultra-modern, smart and comfortable stadium. Even fans who missed the more traditional Highfield Road ground began to warm to what the Ricoh could offer: unrestricted views, leg-room and a decent roof! Complete with its on-site hotel and casino, exhibition halls, a restaurant the length of the pitch and even throw-in sponsors – the Ricoh Arena leaves no commercial stone left unturned.

While the grounds and the times have changed, the pleasure of going along to watch has not. Both the old and new stadiums have witnessed most things that the footballing gods could conjure up. Great games, great players, great despair and great joy have been as regular visitors to Highfield Road and the Ricoh Arena as the City faithful themselves, and long may they remain so!

CITY LEGENDS – CLARRIE BOURTON

For a time in the 1930s, Coventry City were one of the highest scoring teams in the country. In four seasons out of five, from 1932 to 1936, City passed 100 league goals in each season and they became renowned for being an exciting, attack-minded team. Manager Harry Storer wanted a team full of goals, and he got one, thanks in no small measure to Clarrie Bourton, who went on to become the club's all-time leading scorer, with 181 goals in 6 years.

Having suffered a broken leg at Ewood Park, and then been in and out of the Blackburn team, Bourton arrived for £750 in 1931. He went on to make a sensational impact in his opening season; netting seven hat-tricks, including five trebles, plus one 4-goal and one 5-goal haul, along the way to a final tally of 50 strikes (49 in the league and 1 in the FA Cup). Incredibly that year, although City hit 108 league goals, they still only finished half way up the table in twelfth place as they conceded a staggering 97 goals – these figures still remain the highest amounts of goals they have ever scored or conceded in a season.

Football in the 1930s, of course, was very different to the modern era – it was much more about attacking and outscoring your opponents, rather then the pressing and percentage games that dominate today. Combining with fellow forwards Billy Lake and the tricky Jock Lauderdale, Bourton was City's star of the 1930s. A strong, quick centre-forward, he had a powerful shot and terrific finishing ability; he was prolific in each of his first five seasons at City, never dipping below 25 goals. Fans feasted on the number of goals they saw and the chant of the time, 'Come on the Old Five' referred to City's handy habit of regularly putting five past their opponents.

Ironically enough it was only when Harry Storer's men finally achieved the club's first ever promotion, from Division Three South in 1936, that Bourton's goals began to dry up. Whether it was the step up to Division Two, or just the aging process taking its toll, Bourton never quite managed to perform as well at a higher level.

Within little over a year, Bourton was leaving for pastures new, but now, almost seven decades later, his legacy as City's most prolific goalscorer remains intact; no-one has ever got within 50 goals of Bourton's total. In the pantheon of City strikers, the Bantams' star man remains head and shoulders above the rest.

OLDEN, BUT GOLDEN

At 43 years of age, Alf Wood became City's oldest ever player. He achieved that distinction in his second spell at the club when, as an assistant trainer, he stepped in as cover to play in an FA Cup defeat against Plymouth. Not too far behind Wood, was City's most famous custodian, Steve Ogrizovic. At 42, Oggy became City's oldest top-flight player when he made his farewell appearance in May 2000 (a 4–1 thumping of Sheffield Wednesday). Ogrizovic's role at the club changed in his last two years on the playing staff, when he became Magnus Hedman's deputy. It was still testament to his outstanding fitness and longevity that he could even be considered for Premiership football at an age when most people are becoming reconciled to the onset of middle age.

Strangely though, the impressive feats of both Wood and Ogrizovic were almost superseeded on the list of Sky Blue Oldies. In the summer of 1995, Ron Atkinson decided City could do with some experienced back up for the injured Ogrizovic and his up–and-coming young deputy, John Filan. Experience was exactly what Atkinson got in the shape of ex-England stopper Peter Shilton, then a veteran of almost 1,000 league matches, and a mere 45 years of age. Shilton kept the subs' bench warm on a glorious August evening against Manchester City, but was never called upon to play competitively, leaving Alf Wood's record in tact.

STRIKING A CHORD

Ex-City striker Dion Dublin has recently added to the many reasons he achieved fame for. Not content with a top-class career spanning two full decades and four England caps, City's leading top-flight scorer has added another string to his bow by planning, designing and producing a completely new musical instrument – the DUBE.

This percussion instrument is proving a hit, with both schools and the RSC employing it. Dublin has long had a well-documented love of music, early in his career he learnt how to play the saxophone while nursing a broken leg at Manchester United! Stories that Dion's love of music came from his Showaddywaddy-based father were, however, wide of the mark – Dion denies any connections with the 1970s hitmakers.

BIGMOUTH STRIKES AGAIN

When Mick Quinn arrived in the autumn of 1992, very quickly goals followed. With 2 against Liverpool and 2 more in a Boxing Day thrashing of Aston Villa, Quinn was left with 10 goals in his first 6 matches – he was the talk of the Premiership. By the end of that season in Sky Blue the big man weighed in with 17 strikes which, combined with his less-than-svelte figure, had helped him achieve a cult status.

Although Quinn hit a brilliant opening-day hat-trick at Highbury the following August (as Arsenal, the double cup winners, were roasted 3–0), his flow of goals, sadly, began to dry up. A year later he left for Greece, but his playing days were all but done. During his initial prolific spell at Coventry, Quinn had also shown himself to be adept at one-liners for the media, labelling himself the 'fastest player over a yard' in the Premiership, and revelling in his 'Sumo' nickname.

Quinn has since travelled a long way from those early days of being a media favourite, via a racehorse training career, to now becoming one of the most recognised and popular voices on national sports radio station, Talksport. His characteristic breezy delivery, quick-fire opinions and ease with the callers, aligned to his footballing knowledge, have made Quinn the pundit a better bet to stay the course than Quinn the striker, who once set the Premiership on fire.

BACKHANDERS

When Coventry City proudly joined the Football League on 30 August 1919, hopes were high. Although things started badly with a 5–0 home reversal against Spurs, no-one could predict quite how bad they were to get. City lost their first 9 games and did not win until their 20th game, on Christmas Day. A long-standing club tradition of desperately trying to avoid the drop was immediately up and running!

With two games left, City were second bottom and re-election was looming large. They played top-six outfit Bury in both of their last two matches and managed a draw and a final-day win. The 2–1 win over the Shakers brought an escape from the dreaded re-election process, but the game was to go down in club history for all the wrong reasons.

On the surface, City had done fantastically well to turn a 1–0 half-time deficit into a status-securing win. However, mumblings about the authenticity of the result turned into rumours, and 3 years later those rumours turned into allegations – at an FA inquiry investigating match-fixing. The inquiry found that City and Bury had indeed agreed to fix the matches and four City officials – two directors, manager Harry Pollitt and skipper George Chaplin – were found guilty and given life bans.

CHAMPIONS – THIRD DIVISION SOUTH
1935/36

		P	W	D	L	F	A	Pts
1	Coventry City	42	24	9	9	102	45	57
2	Luton Town	42	22	12	8	81	45	56
3	Reading	42	26	2	14	87	62	54
4	QPR	42	22	9	11	84	53	53
5	Watford	42	20	9	13	80	54	49
6	Crystal Palace	42	22	5	15	96	74	49
7	B & H Albion	42	18	8	16	70	63	44
8	Bournemouth	42	16	11	15	60	56	43
9	Notts County	42	15	12	15	60	57	42
10	Torquay United	42	16	9	17	62	62	41
11	Aldershot	42	14	12	16	53	61	40
12	Millwall	42	14	12	16	58	71	40
13	Bristol City	42	15	10	17	48	59	40
14	Clapton Orient	42	16	6	20	55	61	38
15	Northampton T	42	15	8	19	62	90	38
16	Gillingham	42	14	9	19	66	77	37
17	Bristol Rovers	42	14	9	19	69	95	37
18	Southend United	42	13	10	19	61	62	36
19	Swindon Town	42	14	8	20	64	73	36
20	Cardiff City	42	13	10	19	60	73	36
21	Newport County	42	11	9	22	60	111	31
22	Exeter City	42	8	11	23	59	93	27

City's full record that season:

Home						Away					
P	W	D	L	F	A	W	D	L	F	A	Pts
42	19	1	1	75	12	5	8	8	27	33	57

In the whole of the Football League that season, only Division One champions Sunderland scored more league goals than City. The final total of 102 strikes was bolstered by a near-perfect home record. City scored 5 goals or more in 7 different matches that season, including 6–1, 7–1 and 8–1 successes over QPR, Newport and Crystal Palace. For the fourth year out of five, City scored 70+ league goals at Highfield Road and for the fourth year out of five Clarrie Bourton was top scorer once again, as the team and supporters benefited from manager Harry Storer's attack-minded style.

City secured their first ever championship only on the final day of the 1935/36 season. They lay level on points with Luton Town, though with a better goal average as the final matches were played. Luton's 0–0 draw at QPR meant City could have been promoted with just a point of their own, but they went one better and narrowly squeezed home 2–1 against Torquay to make themselves completely sure of the Third Division South title.

Captain George Mason missed the final game through injury and reputedly spent much of it walking around Gosford Green rather than watching the match which would decide City's season. Only when Mason heard the cheers of the crowd at the final whistle did he allow himself back in to share in the celebrations. After finishing second and third in the previous two years, City had patiently gone about their job of steady improvement; their immediate reward was to be Second Division football, but Storer and co. had the top flight in their sights.

City played three full seasons in the second tier before war broke out and final placings of eighth, fourth and fourth suggest that had he had a little longer, Harry Storer might just have got City into the promised land of Division One some thirty years before Jimmy Hill managed to do so.

EVER THE PRO

When Roy Wegerle arrived at Highfield Road in 1992, as part of an exchange deal with Kevin Gallacher, he probably frustrated the Coventry fans more than he wowed them. He had undeniable quality on the ball, but being in a struggling team and suffering with his own injuries, meant he never hit any great heights in Sky Blue.

Off the field, at that time he was little more than an occasional golfer. As Wegerle's career downgraded though, his interest in golf rose, and to his surprise he found that he wasn't just a decent golfer, he was in fact, an excellent one, close to professional standard.

Wegerle retired from football after representing the USA in the 1998 World Cup and decided to see how far he could get with his golf. Within four years he had earned a spot in a European Tour event, the 2002 Alfred Dunhill Championship, held in Johannesburg and worth £500,000. Although Wegerle never went on to achieve high rankings in professional golf, he remains a rare example of a sportsman capable of competing, at least briefly, at the highest level in two different major sports.

AT SIXES & SEVENS

Though City have enjoyed plenty of 90 minutes when they have dished out the punishment, sad to say they have certainly been on the receiving end many times too. Here are some of the biggest pastings of the last 44 years – since promotion to Division One.

Home
Coventry City 1–6 Liverpool, Division One, 5 May 1990
A sunny end-of-season affair saw a rampant John Barnes

in his pomp; City took an early lead, but champions Liverpool wanted revenge for their only home defeat of the season – to City in November.

Away

Chelsea 6–1 Coventry City, Premier League,
21 October 2000
An early sending-off for rookie keeper Chris Kirkland allowed loanee Alan Miller to play his only game as a Sky Blue. He was kept very busy, particularly by 4-goal Jimmy Floyd Hasselbaink as Chelsea ran riot.

Arsenal 6–1 Coventry City, Division One
11 May 1991
For the second successive season, City finished with a 6–1 lesson from that year's champions. This time though, 4 goals in the last 15 minutes for the Gunners gave the scoreline a slightly flattering gloss.

West Brom 6–1 Coventry City, Division One,
8 October 1968
Second from bottom City endured a difficult season, finally avoiding the drop by a single point. Cup-holders West Brom were just too good for City and 5 second-half strikes, 2 from Wembley hero Jeff Astle, sank City.

Everton 6–0 Coventry City, Division One,
26 November 1977
Goodison Park saw second-placed Everton take on fourth-placed City in a top-of-table clash. The Sky Blues were trailing just 1–0 until the 43rd minute and a thrashing was not on the horizon. Bob Latchford, though, sneaked 2 more before half time and then added a third as Everton enjoyed a day when everything went their way.

West Brom 7–1 Coventry City, Division One,
21 October 1978
This famous meltdown at The Hawthorns became as
notorious for the chocolate-brown strip City wore as for
the margin of victory. West Brom enjoyed a vintage year,
finishing third, and with Robson, Regis and Cunnigham
in full flow, City were blown away.

Southampton 8–2 Coventry City, Division One,
28 April 1984
Bobby Gould's team of lower-league leading-lights
were in serious danger of being snuffed out completely
after this disaster at The Dell. Future cup-winner Lloyd
McGrath debuted as it rained goals; City achieved the
rare distinction of conceding hat-tricks to two players,
Danny Wallace and Steve Moran, in one match.

In the decade since City were relegated from the Premier
League, they have not conceded more than 5 in a match
at the time of going to print. Strangely, though, their
old nemesis West Bromwich Albion have once again
inflicted their heaviest defeats of the decade – 5–0 in a
league match at The Hawthorns in December 2006, and
another 5–0 in the FA Cup fifth round tie in front of an
almost full Ricoh Arena, in February 2008.
   If you delve further back into the record books, City
have suffered some even heavier defeats, being hit for
double figures on two occasions:

1901 Berwick Rangers 11–2 Coventry City
FA Cup second qualifying round

1930 Norwich City 10–2 Coventry City
Division Three South

OPERATION PREMIERSHIP

In a bid to galvanise the club and its supporters, erstwhile Managing Director Paul Fletcher launched a bold initiative in 2006, aimed at securing promotion back to the top flight within three years – Operation Premiership. Though sometimes derided for its corporate-speak title and presentational hyperbole, the plan could not have been simpler.

Fletcher aimed to attract new investment in the club, which would in turn be transferred to Micky Adams' team. By then, the club had their much-vaunted new stadium, so all that was missing was the team and opposition to grace it. While cash, enthusiasm and spirits were raised, unfortunately, the team was not. After the promising second half of the 2005/06 season, which saw City finish in a respectable eighth spot, things faltered the following year and first Adams, in January 2007, and then Fletcher in October of that year, left the club.

With Fletcher's departure and the continued fluctuations on the field, it was tempting for some fans to rechristen Operation Premiership as Operation Sinking Ship, but though the plans never came to fruition, there is little doubting the positive intent that lay within them. By today's standards of patience in football, Fletcher's 3-year timescale for City to get back to the big time seems almost a lifetime.

While it is true that the best laid schemes of mice and men often go wrong, it is probably equally true to say without the scheme in the first place you will not get too far. City certainly did need a man with a plan, and not too long after Fletcher's demise, another knowledgeable ex-pro, Ray Ranson, took over the helm, with plans of his own.

COVENTRY CITY'S PLAYING RECORD
1919–2011

Season	League	P	W	D	L	F	A	Pts	Pos
1919/20	Div 2	42	9	11	22	35	73	29	20th
1920/21	Div 2	42	12	11	19	39	70	35	21st
1921/22	Div 2	42	12	10	20	51	60	34	20th
1922/23	Div 2	42	15	7	20	46	63	37	18th
1923/24	Div 2	42	11	13	18	52	68	35	19th
1924/25	Div 2	42	11	9	22	45	84	31	22nd
1925/26	Div 3N	42	16	6	20	73	82	38	16th
1926/27	Div 3S	42	15	7	20	71	86	37	15th
1927/28	Div 3S	42	11	9	22	67	96	31	20th
1928/29	Div 3S	42	14	14	14	62	57	42	11th
1929/30	Div 3S	42	19	9	14	88	73	47	6th
1930/31	Div 3S	42	16	9	17	75	65	41	14th
1931/32	Div 3S	42	18	8	16	108	97	44	12th
1932/33	Div 3S	42	19	6	17	106	77	44	6th
1933/34	Div 3S	42	21	12	9	100	54	54	2nd
1934/35	Div 3S	42	21	9	12	86	50	51	3rd
1935/36	Div 3S	42	24	9	9	102	45	57	1st
1936/37	Div 2	42	17	11	14	66	54	45	8th
1937/38	Div 2	42	20	12	10	66	45	52	4th
1938/39	Div 2	42	21	8	13	62	45	50	4th
1939/40	Div 2	3	1	2	0	8	6	4	4th
SECOND WORLD WAR									
1946/47	Div 2	42	16	13	13	66	59	45	8th
1947/48	Div 2	42	14	13	15	59	52	41	10th
1948/49	Div 2	42	15	7	20	55	64	37	16th
1949/50	Div 2	42	13	13	16	55	55	39	12th
1950/51	Div 2	42	19	7	16	75	59	45	7th
1951/52	Div 2	42	14	6	22	59	82	34	21st
1952/53	Div 3S	46	19	12	15	77	62	50	6th
1953/54	Div 3S	46	18	9	19	61	56	45	14th
1954/55	Div 3S	46	18	11	17	67	59	47	9th

Season	League	P	W	D	L	F	A	Pts	Pos
1955/56	Div 3S	46	20	9	17	73	60	49	8th
1956/57	Div 3S	46	16	12	18	74	84	44	16th
1957/58	Div 3S	46	13	13	20	61	81	39	19th
1958/59	Div 4	46	24	12	10	84	47	60	2nd
1959/60	Div 3	46	21	10	15	78	63	52	4th
1960/61	Div 3	46	16	12	18	80	83	44	15th
1961/62	Div 3	46	16	11	19	64	71	43	14th
1962/63	Div 3	46	18	17	11	83	69	53	4th
1963/64	Div 3	46	22	16	8	98	61	60	1st
1964/65	Div 2	42	17	9	16	72	70	43	10th
1965/66	Div 2	42	20	13	9	73	53	53	3rd
1966/67	Div 2	42	23	13	6	74	43	59	1st
1967/68	Div 1	42	9	15	18	51	71	33	20th
1968/69	Div 1	42	10	11	21	46	64	31	20th
1969/70	Div 1	42	19	11	12	58	48	49	6th
1970/71	Div 1	42	16	10	16	37	38	42	10th
1971/72	Div 1	42	9	15	18	44	67	33	18th
1972/73	Div 1	42	13	9	20	40	55	35	19th
1973/74	Div 1	42	14	10	18	43	54	38	16th
1974/75	Div 1	42	12	15	15	51	62	39	14th
1975/76	Div 1	42	13	14	15	47	57	40	14th
1976/77	Div 1	42	10	15	17	48	59	35	19th
1977/78	Div 1	42	18	12	12	75	62	48	7th
1978/79	Div 1	42	14	16	12	58	68	44	10th
1979/80	Div 1	42	16	7	19	56	66	39	15th
1980/81	Div 1	42	13	10	19	48	68	36	16th
1981/82	Div 1	42	13	11	18	56	62	50	14th
1982/83	Div 1	42	13	9	20	48	59	48	19th
1983/84	Div 1	42	13	11	18	57	77	50	19th
1984/85	Div 1	42	15	5	22	47	64	50	18th
1985/86	Div 1	42	11	10	21	48	71	43	17th
1986/87	Div 1	42	17	12	13	50	45	63	10th
1987/88	Div 1	40	13	14	13	46	53	53	10th
1988/89	Div 1	38	14	13	11	47	42	55	7th

Season	League	P	W	D	L	F	A	Pts	Pos
1989/90	Div 1	38	14	7	17	39	59	49	12th
1990/91	Div 1	38	11	11	16	42	49	44	16th
1991/92	Div 1	42	11	11	20	35	44	44	19th
1992/93	Prem	42	13	13	16	52	57	52	15th
1993/94	Prem	42	14	14	14	43	45	56	11th
1994/95	Prem	42	12	14	16	44	62	50	16th
1995/96	Prem	38	8	14	16	42	60	38	16th
1996/97	Prem	38	9	14	15	38	54	41	17th
1997/98	Prem	38	12	16	10	46	44	52	11th
1998/99	Prem	38	11	9	18	39	51	42	15th
1999/00	Prem	38	12	8	18	47	54	44	14th
2000/01	Prem	38	8	10	20	36	63	34	19th
2001/02	Div 1	46	20	6	20	59	53	66	11th
2002/03	Div 1	46	12	14	20	46	62	50	20th
2003/04	Div 1	46	17	14	15	67	54	65	12th
2004/05	Cham	46	13	13	20	61	73	52	19th
2005/06	Cham	46	16	15	15	62	65	63	8th
2006/07	Cham	46	16	8	22	47	62	56	17th
2007/08	Cham	46	14	11	21	52	64	53	21st
2008/09	Cham	46	13	15	18	49	60	54	17th
2009/10	Cham	46	13	15	18	47	64	54	19th
2010/11	Cham	46	14	13	19	54	58	55	18th

Summary

1919/20	elected to Division 2
1925/26	Division 3 (N)
1926–36	Division 3 (S)
1936–52	Division 2
1952–58	Division 3 (S)
1958/59	Division 4
1959–64	Division 3
1964–67	Division 2
1967–2001	Division 1/Premiership
2001–04	Football League Division One
2004–	The Championship

THE ENTERTAINERS – TOMMY HUTCHISON

In not far short of a decade's service, Tommy Hutchison left City fans with many memories of great wing-play. Like a pickpocket in a crowd, it seemed that the Scotsman could almost dribble his way in and out of a defender's back-pocket. For City fans of a certain age, Hutchison became the benchmark to grade all future wingmen by, and few would go on to reach his high standards.

When he arrived from Blackpool in 1972, Hutchison was returning to the top flight he had tasted briefly with the Seasiders the previous year. Questions as to whether he would maintain the form needed for Division One did not last long, though, as Hutch quickly began to thrive. With a burst of pace, fantastic ball-control and a mazy dribbling style, Hutchison was a defender's nightmare. Of course, defenders in the 1970s were not famed for their deft nudges and subtle touches and the penalty Hutch paid for his elegant wing-play was more than a few clattering challenges. Unlike some wingers though, Hutchison never hid; he kept going back for more, and then some more again.

In only the fourth match of his City career, Hutchison ensured a place in City fans' affections courtesy of a startling solo goal he scored against Arsenal at Highbury. Even home fans were brought to their feet after what would, in time, become known as a typical Hutchison dribble, took him past nearly half the Arsenal team before shooting home from a narrow angle.

Within a year of joining City, Hutchison debuted for Scotland and went on to win all of his seventeen Scottish caps during his time with the Sky Blues. A career highlight was Hutchison's two substitute appearances at the 1974 World Cup finals, twice replacing Kenny Dalglish. Scotland's campaign finished in the frustration of being the first World Cup finalists to exit a tournament undefeated and surprisingly for most observers, Hutchison's international career lasted just one more year.

His brief international career was a complete contrast to his longevity as a league performer; he famously played league football with Swansea until he was 43 and retired from the non-league game with Merthyr at the age of 46! His seasons at City probably saw him at the peak of his powers. Though Coventry enjoyed modest success in the 1970s, only twice featuring in the top half of the table, Hutchison at least could be relied upon to dazzle; sublime touches, snaking runs and defenders scrambling for the headache pills became staple fare for Saturday afternoons at Highfield Road.

Personal highlights for Hutch, apart from Highbury '72, were two crucial strikes in the relegation decider against Bristol City in 1977 and a prominent role in Gordon Milne's swashbuckling class of 1977/78. Spearheaded by Wallace and Ferguson, and ably assisted by the wily wingman, City scored 75 league goals that year in a season-long exhibition of how to play attacking football.

A nice footnote to add to Hutchison's City career was his last appearance at Highfield Road, in Michael Gynn's 2005 testimonial. Despite being close to 60, Hutch turned up and turned on the style once more, giving younger fans a glimpse of still nimble feet and allowing older fans to rewind to their youth. In his pomp, Hutchison was not just good to watch, he was that rarest of things – thrilling.

SKY BLUE CULTURE

For many years now, members of the public have been subjected to a series of both overt and covert references to the Sky Blues in all manner of odd places . . .

An early television reference to the Sky Blues was from a 1970 Monty Python sketch, pointing out the fact that City had never won the FA Cup. By the time City put this matter right, the Pythons had long since slithered off our screens.

Although it is true that Steve Ogrizovic has not often been spotted at the cutting edge of British comedy, it was a position he briefly found himself in a couple of Christmases ago. When the 2008 Christmas special of *Gavin and Stacey* aired, Sky Blue fans the length of the nation were woken from their post-turkey torpor as it was revealed that the show's formidable Welsh stopper, Nessa, knew Ogrizovic from when she used to coach the Coventry City goalkeepers! Although Oggy denied all knowledge of this, one or two jokers did point to the comedy value of some of the keepers employed between Oggy and Keiren Westwood.

City fans were treated to the rare sight of Sky Blue shirts being paraded on our national screens in the ITV drama series *Hearts and Bones* in 2000 and 2001. The series charted the course of a group of Coventry friends who left home for London. References to the Sky Blues were dotted across several episodes, the most memorable of which may have been the sight of actress Amanda Holden in a figure-hugging, Subaru-sponsored, City shirt. Sadly, this bid to raise the country's consciousness of all things Sky Blue took a turn for the worse as the show coincided with City's first ever relegation from the top flight!

In a bid to showcase a large slice of the Coventry's popular culture, the spring of 2003 saw the Herbert Art Gallery host *The Sky Blue Heaven Exhibition*. The room was brim-full of City memorabilia, nostalgia and trivia. The range seemed to cover everything a Sky Blues nut could wish for. From old replica shirts and match programmes, to the suit John Sillett wore at Wembley, there was a glut of Sky Blue paraphernalia to feast upon. The inclusion of two or three rows of Highfield Road bucket-seats plus a life-size football goal added to the fun, and many Sky Blue faithful enjoyed a pleasant meander down Memory Lane.

YOUTH CUP FINALS

The Sky Blues have appeared in five Youth Cup finals, stretching back over 40 years. Fortunes have been mixed though, with just one victory in five attempts. Of course, a strong youth team aims to do more than compete for Youth Cup honours; the main idea is to produce players good enough for the first team. Looking through the names of City players who have represented the club in youth finals, there are several who did go on to make quite an impression.

1967/68 Burnley v Coventry City (1–2, 2–0)
In City's inaugural season in the top flight, the youth team reached the club's first Youth Cup final; proof that the policy of developing younger talent was working. Willie Carr starred in the team before going on to make over 250 senior appearances for City.

1969/70 Tottenham Hotspur v Coventry City (1–0, 0–1, 2–2 and 1–0)
This lengthy tussle was settled only after a second replay in which future Scotland and Liverpool star Graeme Souness scored the winner. Characteristically, Souness also earned a red card for some robust challenges against a City team which fielded defender Jimmy Homes and goalkeeper David Icke, future stars of very different kinds!

1986/87 Coventry City v Charlton Athletic (1–1, 1–0)

The Wednesday before the Sky Blues played Tottenham in the FA Cup final, the youth team provided some hopeful omens by winning the trophy for the first time in the club's history. A Steve Livingstone header decided the destination of the trophy in front of 12,000 delighted home fans, who were merely warming up for the celebrations to follow on the Saturday! Both Livingstone and Tony Dobson started their professional careers at City, making appearances in each of the next four seasons for the first team.

1998/99 West Ham United v Coventry City (3–0, 6–0)

This City team met a highly regarded West Ham team who could boast future England stars Michael Carrick and Joe Cole in their ranks. From that early age Cole was considered an outstanding prospect and his trickery allied to Carrick's impressive ability to find a pass, meant the City boys endured a tortuous 180 minutes. City fielded some future Premiership players of their own in Kirkland, Davenport and McSheffrey, but the tie was one-sided from start to finish.

1999/2000 Arsenal v Coventry City (3–1, 2–0)

Just twelve months later City were back at the top table of youth football again, and although the trophy eluded them, there was a lot of satisfaction to be taken from the level of players coming through the youth ranks. Added to Davenport and McSheffrey from the previous year's campaign came more players who would graduate to the first team: Gary Montgomery, Craig Pead, Lee Fowler as well as the more experienced Craig Strachan.

'WE CAN SEE YOU SNEAKING OUT'

If you ever heard the line, 'We can see you sneaking out', echoing around Highfield Road, you could be sure that someone had taken an almighty beating. When, on 28 November 1990, City fans began to regale Nottingham Forest fans with that very line it was a signal that it was Forest who had suffered the pummelling. Incredibly, the chorus rang out after barely half an hour of this League Cup fourth round tie as City raced into a 4–0 lead and hundreds of Forest fans flooded out of the stadium with just under an hour still to play; they were to miss out on a feast of a game.

City were superb for 35 minutes. Cyrille Regis led the line smartly, combining with Kevin Gallacher and Steve Livingstone to help City race to a 4-goal advantage. The pick of the goals was a delightful chip from Gallacher as he raced onto a defence-splitting ball from Regis, and by the time the wide man had completed his hat-trick it looked a certainty that Forest's two-year reign as League Cup holders was over; they were surely dead and buried. Forest's number nine, Nigel Clough, had other ideas. He replied with a 7-minute hat-trick of his own before the interval to leave City reeling, and the tie wide open.

Within 10 minutes of the restart Forest had levelled through Garry Parker and the best comeback since Lazarus was unfolding before a disbelieving Highfield Road. City players looked as downcast as Forest's were uplifted; momentum had switched to Brian Clough's men. Football though, being the cruellest of games, had another twist or two left. Rookie striker Steve Livingstone got his head to a Regis shot to put City 5–4 ahead and despite Forest swarming forward they could not find the net until Steve Hodge's last-minute strike.

Coventry players and fans were in momentary despair until they realised the goal would not be allowed to stand due to an infringement.

One of the matches of this, or any season, finally finished in City's favour, a 5–4 thriller. A fantastic, tortuous and completely thrilling match for City fans was even tougher for the Forest fans who stayed to witness it all, and who by the final whistle, perhaps wished they had exited an hour earlier to the strains of, 'We can see you sneaking out'!

CITY'S BEST FA CUP RUNS – PART I

1909/10

Qualifying 5	(A)	Kettering	5–0
Round 1	(A)	Preston North End	2–1
Round 2	(A)	Portsmouth	1–0
Round 3	(H)	Nottingham Forest	3–1
Quarter-Final	(H)	Everton	0–2

City's first foray into the latter stages of the FA Cup came when they were a non-league outfit, still plying their trade in the Southern League. Coventry's first round tie against Preston was the club's first ever competitive match against a team from the First Division and despite being clear underdogs, City came from behind to win 2–1.

After overcoming fellow Southern Leaguers Portsmouth in the second round, top-flight Nottingham Forest were the next visitors to Highfield Road. City installed extra seats and raised the admission prices for the match against a struggling Forest whose porous defence had leaked goals all season. That trend continued as an inspired City triumphed 3–1 in front of over 12,000 fans, double the average crowd. A glamorous quarter-final against Everton brought a dilemma for the club; the choice was between playing at home again or switching to a larger ground for larger revenue. After some debate, City resisted the temptation to move, doubling the admission instead! Sadly though, home advantage counted for little as Everton's more experienced team came through 2–0.

Although it was to be over 50 years until Coventry next reached the last eight of the cup, the 1910 team helped get the club noticed and, more importantly, the cup run raised money to for a new stand a year later.

ALL SIT DOWN ...

In 1981, under Jimmy Hill's stewardship, the Sky Blues embarked on the ground-breaking venture of turning Highfield Road into English football's first all-seater stadium. It was the year that local band The Specials had just christened the city 'Ghost Town' and for good reason – Coventry was in the grip of an almighty economic recession with jobs disappearing from the city at an alarming rate.

The thinking behind the new policy was simple enough; to reduce, and then eliminate, hooliganism by pricing out the troublemakers and appealing to a 'family audience'. Of course these aims were widely welcomed, as the 1970s had seen an increase in disturbances nationally, and Highfield Road had not escaped. Too often the post-match ritual had included a quick dash across Gosford Park or Hillfields to avoid opposing fans who were not looking for a cultural exchange. The prevailing view in City's boardroom was not just that something had to be done, but that only wide-ranging changes could cut out the hooliganism.

The changes which were introduced were radical; all terraced areas were replaced with seats, while most prices increased greatly. The idea of the all-seater stadium had been pioneered in Scotland with some success by Aberdeen, but the Dons team of the time was winning trophies, both domestically and in Europe – a sharp contrast with City who hovered between fourteenth and nineteenth for seven straight years.

Mixed performances on the field and inflated prices were never likely to do much for attendances in the new-look Highfield Road, and sure enough they didn't. The 1980/81 average crowd of just short of 17,000 plummeted to a little over 13,000 within a year of the all-seat experiment. Funnily enough, City had been prepared to take a hit on their attendances as they thought the smaller crowds would generate more revenue and that is exactly what happened. The fall in home attendances was complemented by a rise in gate receipts of 15 per cent. Though things may have looked good on the balance sheet, the subsequent dip, and then disappearance of any atmosphere was blamed solely on the introduction of seats. The enjoyment of watching live football was dramatically reduced, as Highfield Road became a noise-free zone.

Fighting falling crowds was one problem, but City had other fights on their mind too. Within a month of the seats being installed, Leeds United fans proved that seats could be ripped out and used as frisbees. Rather than the old trouble disappearing, it seemed that there were simply new ways for some fans to get up to their old tricks.

With the benefit of hindsight, it is possible to point out several of the blunders City made. Asking fans to sit down without a roof on the open East Terrace was never likely to be good for business. Also, the idea that fans would automatically behave well if they were sitting down, seems naïve. Of all the mistakes City made though, arguably the biggest blunder was in the pricing policy.

Prices rose steeply for the new stadium. Whereas a West End terrace ticket had cost £1.50 in the year before the all-seater, the price suddenly doubled to £3. Worse was to follow. Part of the pricing strategy was the £5 on-the-day ticket. The idea was to inconvenience hooligans, by requiring them to buy the cheaper tickets in advance; however, the actual effect was that the casual supporter was lost to the club. Nobody could choose to go to the match on the day without being hit financially, so, nobody bothered. Record-breaking unemployment figures of three million, might have told some clubs that price hikes were a bad idea, but not City! With the dole queues lengthening and local factories closing down, it was simply not the time for prices to go through the roof.

Attendances continued to nosedive and at the end of the second season, crowds were averaging a paltry 10,500, figures which were regarded as appalling. After two seasons of no terraces, City officials admitted defeat; their costly, all-seater experiment had failed. For the start of the 1983/84 season, fans were again allowed to stand at Highfield Road as the Spion Kop was partially opened to card-carrying home fans.

CITY'S BEST LEAGUE CUP RUNS – PART I

Although yet to appear in a League Cup final, City have enjoyed some memorable runs in the competition.

1964/65

Round 2	(H)	Ipswich Town	4–1
Round 3	(H)	Mansfield Town	3–2
Round 4	(H)	Sunderland	4–2
Quarter-Final	(H)	Leicester City	1–8

The tournament was still in its infancy, but hopes that City might progress to a first major final were unceremoniously dashed as top-flight Leicester ran riot. Though injury to George Curtis did not help, a gulf in class was hard to deny as City suffered the heaviest home defeat in their history.

1970/71

Round 2	(A)	Tranmere Rovers	1–1
Replay	(H)	Tranmere Rovers	2–1
Round 3	(H)	West Ham United	3–1
Round 4	(H)	Derby County	1–0
Quarter-final	(A)	Tottenham Hotspur	1–4

A strong Tottenham team had too much firepower for City. Martin Chivers netted a hat-trick as Spurs' cup run continued. The Londoners went all the way to Wembley where they beat Aston Villa to lift the trophy.

1973/74

Round 2	(H)	Darlington	5–1
Round 3	(A)	Bristol City	2–2
Replay	(H)	Bristol City	2–1
Round 4	(H)	Stoke City	2–1
Quarter-final	(H)	Manchester City	2–2
Replay	(A)	Manchester City	2–4

City twice led in an exciting replay at Maine Road, but once again the quarter-finals proved to be the stumbling block. Man City went on to Wembley, but Norwich won the cup.

DID YOU KNOW?

Playing by the Rules
Probably the most famous goal in Coventry City history (until Keith Houchen donned wings and flew to head home his spectacular Cup final goal) was one which was to become outlawed soon afterwards – the Donkey Kick.

In October 1970, the Sky Blues hosted champions Everton and went on to win 3–1 in one of the season's better displays. At the time it was just another game between two middling sides; there was nothing particularly memorable until the 80th minute when something truly extraordinary happened. From an advanced City free-kick, midfield schemer Willie Carr might have been expected to cross the ball into a crowded penalty area, hoping for a goalbound nudge or deflection, or failing that he might have rolled a short pass into a team-mate's path, for him to try his luck from distance. Carr did neither of the expected options; instead, he flicked the ball up vertically between his heels, for the onrushing Ernie Hunt to simply volley the ball over the Everton wall and past keeper Rankin. This simple idea with the deadly execution left Everton gobsmacked and City jubilant.

The man credited with the idea for the kick was City coach Bill Asprey, who passed it on to Carr and Hunt in pre-season and the Everton game in early October saw its successful first attempt. Sadly, the audacious move was not to live for long in the game as FIFA outlawed the innovation, insisting that the ball must travel its whole circumference from any free-kick. Luckily however, the *Match of the Day* cameras were on hand to record the strike, and judging from the number of reruns of the goal, the sheer wit and daring of the Donkey Kick make it as popular today as ever.

You're having a laugh!

On 6 April 1997, the Sky Blues lay in desperate relegation trouble, fixed to the bottom of the table and facing title-chasing Liverpool at Anfield – things looked bleak. It was the year Gordon Strachan took over the reins from Ron Atkinson, but City had continued to struggle all season. Although Atkinson had 'moved upstairs' to become a Director of Football, he was invited along to help the team prepare for the Anfield trip.

There are many ways for professional sportsmen to prepare for a significant fixture: intensive repetitive drills, dedicated fitness regimes, or embrace all that the latest sports science and psychology can offer. On the other hand, you could ditch all of that, take a leaf out of Ron Atkinson's book of man-management, and call for a lovable, old school, scouse comedian, say Stan Boardman, to lighten the mood prior to kick-off!

Big Ron decided City's players needed to relax, and certainly if they spent too much time looking at Liverpool's team sheet, replete with stellar names Fowler, McManaman and Barnes, the nerves would have jangled. Instead, the Sky Blues' own Mr Bojangles seemed to have called it right as City stole a 2–1 win with a late Dion Dublin winner coming from a comical piece of goalkeeping from David James. Quite what lines Stan Boardman came up with have never entered the public domain, but the funny bones he reached clearly did the trick.

Interestingly, the Sky Blues' pre-match comedy was not the first occasion a City manager had turned to a Liverpudlian comic to lighten the mood before a big match. Way back in April 1964, Jimmy Hill had brought Jimmy Tarbuck into the dressing room to relax the team before the promotion-clincher against Colchester. That day Tarby worked his own magic and City won thanks to a George Hudson goal.

King of the Diddy Men

On the subject of helpful scousers it would be remiss to overlook Knotty Ash's own royalty, Ken Dodd. Prior to kick-off before the 1963 FA Cup quarter-final at home to Manchester United, Doddy appeared on the pitch at Highfield Road wearing a Sky Blue shirt.

Quite what the logic of this was is hard to fathom, as the home fans were already in a state of huge excitement as the Third Division Sky Blues took on mighty Manchester United, and this only days after a monumental cup upset against Sunderland. Whatever the reason for Dodd's appearance, it quickly soured as the master of the tickling stick took off his City shirt to then reveal . . . a United one! Dodd did escape the baying crowds and, well into his 80s, continues to tickle the nation's funnybone, although as far as the author is aware though, he is yet to make a return appearance to any City game!

CITY LEGENDS – GEORGE CURTIS

George Curtis' statistics are impressive: he played 543 first-team matches; he was one of a select group of players who played in all four divisions for the first team; he was the record appearance holder for nearly 30 years. Impressive though the stats are, they do not tell half the story of the man City fans knew and loved as the 'Iron Man'.

George Curtis was tough when he played for City and he was tough before he even arrived. Aged just 15, Curtis had worked for 9 months down the pits in Kent, ensuring he already knew plenty about hard graft and team work. Curtis was spotted playing for a colliery team and invited to Highfield Road for a trial, and after making an early impression he debuted at 16 against Newport.

Curtis was an established part of the City team before Jimmy Hill arrived in late 1961 and he was to remain so for almost all of the most successful decade in the club's history, captaining the team through two promotion campaigns. Curtis' uncompromising style earned him the 'Iron Man' nickname, but it was less a case of sheer brute force and more a case of his robustness, and his iron will to win. Despite his reputation for sometimes rugged defending, Curtis was never sent off in a first-team match for the Sky Blues.

Football in the 1960s, with all its physicality, is very far removed from the modern game in which players are much more protected; what does remain constant though is the need for a successful team to have a leader, and for City that leader was George Curtis. His physical strength, his determination to win and his ability to crunch a tackle made him an opponent to be feared and an inspiration to his team. In the heart of the City defence, he was a colossus.

Sadly, after playing such a pivotal role in City's ascent up the league, Curtis broke a leg in only his second match in the First Division and missed most of that first season up. He did recover to play nearly 50 top-flight games in the next two years, before signing for rivals Aston Villa.

Although Curtis' playing career for City ended in December 1969, he returned to the club in a variety of key background roles, working first as commercial manager, before later joining the board of directors.

When Don Mackay's reign as manager finally hit the rocks in the spring of 1986, City had three games left to secure their top-flight status. The club needed someone with knowledge, experience and preferably a passion for Coventry City – they asked George Curtis to help out. He agreed to the request so long as his old team-mate John Sillett, then the youth team coach, was part of the new-look management team.

The Iron Man had certainly not gone rusty in his time away from first-team matters, as the team won two out of three matches to secure City's survival once again. Curtis and Sillett were then given the reins for the 1986/87 season and a glorious chapter in the club's history was about to begin. Curtis' commercial expertise and discipline, allied to Sillett's coaching acumen, seemed to make the ideal management pairing and immediately results improved with City staying in the top half of the league all year.

Once the FA Cup run started, the season got better and better of course and City went on to reach heights that had only been dreamed of before. Players of the time talk of Curtis and Sillett's man-management skills setting them apart. Indeed, there are several stories of how George Curtis rigorously maintained standards, with a tweak of a nose here, or the nibble of an ear there! However he did it though, Curtis made sure the 1987 vintage were disciplined, organised and ready to overcome any challenges put in front of them – just as he had been two decades before.

Throughout his long career with Coventry City, both playing and managing, Curtis could certainly be called a Sky Blue hero, in what was very often a sky-high time.

THE HITMEN

The leading goalscorers for Coventry City:

1	Clarrie Bourton	182 goals in 241 games	(1931–37)
2	Billie Lake	123 goals in 244 games	(1928–39)
3	Ted Roberts	86 goals in 222 games	(1936–52)
4	Ray Straw	87 goals in 158 games	(1957–61)
5	Frank Herbert	86 goals in 199 games	(1922–29)
6	Peter Hill	78 goals in 309 games	(1948–62)
7	George Hudson	75 goals in 129 games	(1963–66)
8	Leslie Jones	73 goals in 145 games	(1934–37)
9	Dion Dublin	71 goals in 171 games	(1994–98)
10	Jock Lauderdale	63 goals in 182 games	(1931–36)
11	Cyrille Regis	62 goals in 282 games	(1984–91)
12	Ian Wallace	60 goals in 140 games	(1976–80)

A quick trawl through the list shows that the number of modern-day strikers in the list is comparatively low. More recent players, especially sought-after goalscorers like Ian Wallace and Dion Dublin, become so in demand that they do not tend to stay for very long at clubs. Also, it is probably fair to say that modern football has much better organised defences nowadays which make scoring harder, than in days gone by. The City team of the 1930s with super strikers Clarrie Bourton and Billy Lake often fielded five forwards, and incredibly managed to score over 100 league goals in four out of five seasons – a golden era indeed!

SKY BLUE DAYS

The modern Sky Blue era began with the 1962 appointment of Jimmy Hill. With two promotions in 5 years, Hill brought about the success that everyone craved, but he made more than just a winning team. Off the pitch, Hill's innovations transformed Coventry City into a modern, forward-thinking, commercially smart club; he quite literally turned the place Sky Blue . . .

For the start of the 1962/63 season a new all sky blue kit, was launched, a new era was clearly starting.

When the *Coventry Evening Telegraph* reported on a 1962 friendly against Birmingham, the new-look Coventry City got a new nickname, and the 'Sky Blues' were born.

The 'Sky Blue Special' took fans to away games, with beer, music and post-match interviews along the way.

Sky Blue Rose was the 1960s equivalent of today's club websites; if you phoned up Rose McNulty you could find out up-to-date information and news from the Sky Blues camp.

Sky Blue Pools raised much-needed money for the club with thousands of weekly contributors.

In addition, other firsts in the 1960s included:

The first electronic scoreboard in the country arrived courtesy of the *Evening Telegraph* in 1964.

The first closed-circuit television broadcast took place on 6 October 1965 for the Sky Blues' away match at Cardiff City. Four large screens at Highfield Road showed the game live to over 10,000 fans as City began to explore the possibilities of live matches.

The first 'Pop and Crisps' parties were launched in 1961 for younger fans to meet their heroes and forge stronger links with the club. Decades later, the Sky Blues continue to hold Christmas parties and open days for fans, still encouraging new fans to join in.

THE CREAKING GATE

Throughout City's top-flight years they often went desperately close to dropping down only to miraculously claw their way back to safety. Although the football wasn't always top-drawer, the thrills and spills of the various relegation battles did provide fans with more edge-of-the-seat moments than the average rollercoaster. Three consecutive seasons in the mid-1980s provided a purple patch for perilous positions, and a blueprint for how to get out of them . . .

A LICK OF PAINT

The 1983/84 season was a tumultuous one from start to finish. Bobby Gould's many new signings exceeded all expectations, their 4–0 annihilation of champions Liverpool was one of City's most startling top-flight results. At about that time though, the wheels careered off the Sky Blue bandwagon and the team went from forward to reverse gears in the blink of an eye. A dreadful run of one win in eighteen league matches led to a steady drop down the table with the team hitting rock-bottom in a terrifying 8–2 defeat at Southampton. It seemed impossible that Bobby Gould could ever engineer a way out of the wreckage of the season.

By the time Norwich arrived on the last day, for the Sky Blues it was win, and hope other results went your way, or bust. Norwich scored first and although loan-signing Ferguson equalised, City were again staring down the barrel. Dave Bennett's second-half strike (debate raged over whether it was brilliant vision, or just a cross that the keeper had made a mess of) put the Sky Blues ahead, but they were far from secure.

In the final minutes another Norwich cross was aimed at the Canaries' young target man, Robert Rosario. He rose, made full contact and nodded the ball past Suckling in the City goal. Just a millimetre's different trajectory would have seen the ball bounce in off the inside of the post and take City down. Instead, the ball bounced back off the inside of the post into the arms of a horrified Suckling, who held on, like a mother with her newborn, for dear life. The margins between success and failure had never been closer; literally, the thickness of a coat of paint had saved City's skins.

NEVER AGAIN

City were not meant to get into such trouble again, but if anything, the predicament they found themselves in just 12 months later was even worse. Postponements due to Easter illnesses meant City's season would finish later than everybody else's, and fans were busy doing their calculations; Norwich City completed their games 8 points clear, but the Sky Blues had three matches left and 9 points left to play for.

The first of the three matches was away at the league's worst team, Stoke City, who had registered just three wins all season. It was no easy ride, though, and after a goalless and nervous first period, Stuart Pearce's second-half penalty put the Sky Blues ahead. Stoke soon had a penalty of their own though; when Ian Painter's shot crashed down off the bar and City breathed again.

The following Thursday night, Luton Town were the visitors to Highfield Road and anything less than maximum points would confirm the Sky Blues' relegation. City pressed and pressed all night long, yet the visitors refused to buckle and the clock was ticking. When Luton's right-back, Tim Breacker, clearly handled in front of referee Stevens, one of the easiest penalty kick awards in the history of Highfield Road was unbelievably not given and the nearly 15,000 fans were beginning to think they were witnessing the cruellest 'one of those nights', where nothing would fall for the Sky Blues.

With just 6 minutes left the unlikeliest combination of players on the pitch conjured up a piece of Sky Blue magic that lived long in the memory. Centre-back Trevor Peake could always tackle with a crunch, but not usually on the left wing. Yet it was there he found himself winning the ball back before delivering a testing ball into the Luton six-yard box. The distinctive figure of Steve Foster made a mess of clearing the ball and City's own strong-arm stopper, Brian Kilcline, launched a rocket that NASA would have approved of into the bottom corner of Les Sealey's net. On the night that Brian Kilcline's own Coventry home was burgled, Peake and Kilcline pinched the points for City, who had just one leg left to complete of a remarkable treble.

A dazzling, sunny Sunday morning saw City welcome champions Everton in the game that would define their season. The Merseysiders had already wrapped up the league, won the Cup Winners' Cup and lost the previous week's FA Cup final; their year's work was almost done. City's players on the other hand, had futures and careers to play for, they could not have been more motivated, they simply had to win.

43

Whatever the state of the players before the game, there was no mistaking the urgency and purpose with which City began. Regis' towering header opened the scoring within 5 minutes and when Micky Adams doubled the lead within 20, the miracle escape was on the way. Though Everton rallied, further goals from Regis and Gibson pulled City clear for a comfortable 4–1 win.

Legend has it that some Norwich players were on the beach and manager Ken Brown walking his dog when news of City's escape came through. However they heard it, the fact that City had had won three games running for the first time all season was headline news; the longest of long shots had been pulled off, and the rallying cry of 'Never Again' echoed out.

THIRD TIME LUCKY

As most of the previous season's team remained, hopes were high that Don Mackay would get more from his players in his first full term in charge. Somehow though, regardless of what faces were coming or going, 1985/86 followed what was becoming an established pattern of occasional highlights, false dawns and a fearful conclusion.

A run of nearly 5 months without a home win meant City could not escape the bottom third of the league all season. When they lost 5–0 at Anfield in April it seemed as if the writing was on the wall once again, this time in permanent marker – City were facing the drop. With three games left Don Mackay left the club and the most experienced men on the staff, youth team manager John Sillett and then record-appearance maker and Executive Director, George Curtis were asked to steer the team to safety.

A win and a defeat in Curtis and Sillett's first two games offered some encouragement, but for the third year in succession, City would have to win their final match to guarantee survival in the First Division. Goalscoring heroes from the previous two seasons' dramas, Kilcline and Bennett, did the trick again as City held on to a narrow 2–1 win over Queens Park Rangers. This time it was the turn of the City crossbar to keep out a late goal-bound effort to ensure safety was reached.

Eight of the team who salvaged survival on that last day in 1986 (it would have been nine but for Brian Borrows' injury), would go on to play another crucial last-match decider 12 months later. Happily, the following year had a very different prize on offer, as underachievement gave way to overachievement and the 1987 FA Cup final was won.

CAN WE PLAY YOU EVERY WEEK?

When a Michael Mifsud-inspired City triumphed 2–0 at Old Trafford in the third round of the League Cup in September 2007, they not only enjoyed a memorable cup upset, but also completed a very unlikely hat-trick. A full 27 years after last playing United in the competition, City made it three wins out of three over the mighty Reds.

Back in 1980/81 Gordon Milne's youthful team embarked on a tremendous League Cup run when they played United in the then two-legged second round tie. Although United were not then the power that they had been for the last couple of decades, they still had star names like Gary Bailey, Lou Macari and Steve Coppell in their side. However, a Tommy English goal secured a 1–0 advantage for City from the Old Trafford game, and the return leg was approached with confidence. At Highfield Road a sweetly struck Andy Blair strike doubled City's aggregate lead, and United, as they never do in the League Cup against City (!), were unable to break down a resolute defence.

CHAMPIONS – DIVISION THREE 1963/64

		P	W	D	L	F	A	Pts
1	Coventry City	46	22	16	8	98	61	60
2	Crystal Palace	46	23	14	9	73	51	60
3	Watford	46	23	12	11	79	59	58
4	Bournemouth	46	24	8	14	79	58	56
5	Bristol City	46	20	15	11	84	64	55
6	Reading	46	21	10	15	79	62	52
7	Mansfield Town	46	20	11	15	76	62	51
8	Hull City	46	16	17	13	73	68	49
9	Oldham Ath	46	20	8	18	73	70	48
10	Peterborough Utd	46	18	11	17	75	70	47
11	Shrewsbury Town	46	18	11	17	73	80	47
12	Bristol Rovers	46	19	8	19	91	79	46
13	Port Vale	46	16	14	16	53	49	46
14	Southend United	46	15	15	16	77	78	45
15	QPR	46	18	9	19	76	78	45
16	Brentford	46	15	14	17	87	80	44
17	Colchester United	46	12	19	15	70	68	43
18	Luton Town	46	16	10	20	64	80	42
19	Walsall	46	13	14	19	59	76	40
20	Barnsley	46	14	15	19	68	94	39
21	Millwall	46	14	10	22	53	67	38
22	Crewe Alexandra	46	11	12	23	50	77	34
23	Wrexham	46	13	6	27	75	107	32
24	Notts County	46	9	9	28	45	92	27

This was the year that Jimmy Hill's Sky Blues began their spectacular climb up the league, winning the Third Division championship. Hill had started to sow the seeds of success the year before by finishing fourth and reaching the FA Cup quarter-finals, but a further year was needed for his new team to blossom fully.

Inspired by George Hudson's 26 goals before the New Year, City went 9 points clear at the top and looked racing certainties for promotion. It was then that the wobble started and the promotion push stalled; City went eleven matches without a win and trailing teams had caught them up. Hudson's second half of the season mirrored the team's, as goals and wins became harder to find.

With one match left just 2 points separated City, Watford and leaders Crystal Palace, one of the three would miss out. While Watford and Palace contrived to lose their final fixtures, City held firm to see off Colchester 1–0 and it was that man Hudson who got the promotion and championship-clinching strike. For the first time in a dozen years City would be back in the second tier of English football and just 3 years later Jimmy Hill would deliver the Sky Blues to Division One.

MONEY, MONEY, MONEY!

Although it is now nearly eleven years since City last broke their own transfer record, the club has often been prepared to take a plunge into the transfer market in a bid to bring success. After winning at Wembley, John Sillett famously declared that City were going to 'shop at Harrods' in the future. However, a look at the list of the top transfer fees City have splashed out, reveals that the goods bought at Harrods do not *always* necessarily bring a guarantee of success!

Largest Transfer Fees paid by Coventry City in the Premiership:

July 2000	Craig Bellamy	£6,500,000
August 1999	Robbie Keane	£6,000,000
July 1999	Mustapha Hadji	£4,000,000

December 1997	Viorel Moldovan	£3,000,000
July 1996	Gary McAllister	£3,000,000
December 1995	Noel Whelan	£2,000,000
September 1994	Dion Dublin	£1,950,000

Largest Transfer Fees paid by Coventry City Decade by Decade:

November 1919	Ted Hannay	£1,100
September 1928	Billy Kirton	£1,300
August 1938	George Ashall	£3,500
October 1949	Martin McDonnell	£12,000
December 1950	Tommy Briggs	£20,000
February 1968	Neil Martin	£90,000
July 1979	Gary Collier	£325,000
October 1989	Kevin Drinkell	£800,000

The inflated fees reflect the increasing commercialisation of the English game, with record fees roughly doubling or trebling each decade. It is impossible to miss the frequency of record fees being paid out in the Premiership seasons though, a time when City had more money to spend than ever before, yet still managed to accrue debts reportedly close to the £60,000,000 mark.

CITY LEGENDS – CYRILLE REGIS

When Cyrille Regis signed for City in the autumn of 1984, he seemed to be a player on the wane; the early promise of the bull-dozing, net-bursting forward had stalled and West Brom cheerfully moved him on for just £300,000.

For the first 2½ years of his time at Highfield Road, Regis did little to dispel the doubters. Long barren runs in front of goal replaced the speedy, scoring ones for which he had been famed, and Regis, it seemed, was a spent force. His plight mirrored the team's; as City continually struggled against relegation, Regis continually struggled to find any form or consistency.

Occasional highlights – 5 goals in a match against Chester and 2 in the relegation decider of 1985 against champions Everton – were not enough to illuminate the gloomy Highfield Road landscape. Only the narrowest of escapes 3 years running kept City and Regis afloat in the top flight and when the double-act of Sillett and Curtis took over, the portents were poor.

John Sillett had the seemingly impossible task of trying to unlock the potential that Regis still offered, yet his solution was so simple it defied belief that no-one had thought of it before. Sillett asked Regis how he wanted the team to play and was told to play to feet with Regis as the focal point of the attack! The simple ploy of playing to the strengths of your best players was then tried and put into action. Eureka!

Regis shone again in the very first home match of Sillett's first season. That 2–1 triumph over Arsenal heralded a very different style of play. City passed short as well as long, but most importantly, they passed accurately and to feet, with Regis as the focal point. When he belted home from 20 yards that night something seemed different; certainly football's biggest smile was back on view.

In a season of wonderful memories for all City fans, one or two Regis moments stand out: the last-minute winner against Spurs in the 4–3 Christmas cracker, in heading a rebound in off the bar; the jet-fuelled acceleration that took him past Sheffield Wednesday's back line in the Cup quarter-final; or, the smile as wide as the Hillsborough Kop, after Leeds were finally beaten in a thrilling semi-final.

While the Wembley triumph of 16 May 1987 became a pivotal moment for every City fan, for Regis the day proved beyond doubt that, once again, he was a forward to be feared. On English fooball's showpiece occasion, Regis bestrode the pitch like a colossus; the strength, determination and verve that defined his early years at West Brom were back on centre stage. Tottenham centre-backs Gary Mabbutt and Richard Gough were outmuscled, outsmarted and finally undone by City's bustling number nine; in a team full of heroes, he was magnificent.

The following years brought further England call-ups and many more top-class performances. While Regis was never the prolific goalscorer a player with his talents could have been, his abilities at leading the line, holding the ball up and linking play were hard to better. Though chances were only regularly converted for maybe 2 or 3 of his 7 years at Highfield Road, Regis still commanded much respect from his peers, and inspired much devotion from his own supporters; not for being an ace goal-grabber perhaps, but rather, for being a fine exponent of the centre-forward's craft.

Regis had everything a forward needed: adhesive ball-control, gladiatorial strength, pace and presence and a nice collection of goals too. As players with his ability have rarely graced City teams over the years, the famous chant of, 'Nice one Cyrille, Let's have another one', always sounded just about right!

RECORD-BREAKERS – GLAZIER & MATTHEWS

When Coventry kid Reg Matthews signed for City straight from Barker Butts School in 1950, he was embarking on a career that would take him to the very top of his goalkeeping trade. From the youth team to the first team, Matthews came through the ranks at City. After appearing first against Southend in 1952/53, he shared the keeping duties with Peter Taylor (of later Clough and Taylor fame) for a couple of seasons before making the number one jersey his own. Although City remained in Division Three South throughout Matthews' time at the club, his reputation quickly grew; he was regarded as an outstanding keeper renowned for his courage, agility and athleticism.

In his final year at City, Matthews achieved the very rare distinction of being called up by, and playing for, England while still a third-tier player. He debuted in front of 134,000 spectators against Scotland in a 1–1 draw, with Pathé News declaring he had played 'splendidly'. Four more caps followed within a year, making Matthews a prized asset. Chelsea had been league champions just one year earlier and eager to maintain their lofty position they paid City £22,000 for Matthews' services – a then world record fee for a goalkeeper. After leaving City, Matthews continued to play with distinction for Chelsea and then Derby over the next decade, but was never selected for his country again – perhaps City fans saw him at his best.

Strange to think of it now, but the Sky Blues once paid a world record fee for a goalkeeper themselves. City had just won the Third Division title the previous season and wanted to continue to progress, so Jimmy Hill bought Bill Glazier from similarly promoted Crystal Palace for £35,000 in 1964.

Buying Glazier gave Hill a top-class keeper, and also sent out a clear signal that Coventry City were serious about their climb up the divisions. Glazier's agility and longevity served City well for ten seasons when, barring injury, he was the first name on the teamsheet. Speaking in 2005, he had fond memories of his time at the club, saying of the promotion-clinching win against Wolves in 1967, 'Coventry have done two things in 106 years, and I was very proud to be involved in one of them.'

THE NUMBERS GAME

It has often been said that statistics never tell the whole of a story, but some Sky Blue stats are hard to ignore . . .

£60,000,000 was the widely quoted figure of how much Coventry City were in debt when they were relegated from the Premier League in 2001

£13,000,000 is the largest transfer fee City have ever received for a player; Inter Milan paid that much for Robbie Keane in the summer of 2000.

£6,500,000 is the largest transfer fee City have ever spent on a player. It was for striker Craig Bellamy who stayed one season in which the club were relegated!

98,000 fans were in Wembley to watch City lift the FA Cup in 1987.

32,609 is the capacity of the Ricoh Arena.

2,059 is Coventry's lowest ever attendance for a home league match; just 2,059 went to watch a Division Three (South) fixture against Crystal Palace. The game, which was played on 13 February 1928, finished in a 2–2 draw.

1898 was the year that Coventry City started life, after Singers FC.

601 is the number of times Steve Ogrizovic kept goal for the Sky Blues, from 1984 to 2000.

297 is the number of games Richard Shaw played before finally scoring for the Sky Blues; his one and only strike came in a memorable 5–2 win at Gillingham in May 2004.

241 consecutive appearances were made by Steve Ogrizovic, from August 1984 to September 1989.

108 is the highest number of league goals Coventry City have ever scored in a single season. The goal glut of 1931/32 was spearheaded by Clarrie Bourton's 49 league strikes (he also scored 1 in the FA Cup).

106 years is how long City's home was at Highfield Road, from 1899 to 2005, spanning three centuries.

82 days without a single goal is City's worst ever run. In their inaugural league season of 1919/20, they went 82 days and eleven matches without a goal – from 4 October to 25 December. The 3–2 Christmas Day win over Stoke was the club's first ever league win.

51 years went by, from February 1937 to November 1988, without City recording a win over local rivals Aston Villa.

50 seasons ago Coventry City were rebranded by Jimmy Hill and the Sky Blues era started.

44 years have passed since the Sky Blues last finished in the top six of any league – this arguably makes Coventry the least successful team in England, as every other club has at least enjoyed one top-six finish in all that time.

25 games was the club's longest ever undefeated run, from November 1966, to the end of the promotion-clinching campaign, in May 1967.

22 seasons running, from 1967 to 1989, Coventry played Liverpool at Anfield and could not win. The Sky Blues finally broke their duck in November 1989; Regis' header from a Greg Downs cross secured the long-awaited 1–0 win.

10 goals in six games was the sensational start Mick Quinn made to his city career in the autumn of 1992. Nearly 60 years before, Arthur Bacon did even better, hitting 14 in his first five games!

9 goals is the most City have ever scored in a match; the record win was 9–0 over Bristol City in Division Three South, 1934.

5 Only three players have ever achieved a nap hand and scored 5 times in a match for City: Clarrie Bourton in a 6–1 win against Bournemouth in 1931; Arthur Bacon in a 7–3 win against Gillingham in 1934; Cyrille Regis in a 7–2 win against Chester in 1985.

4 players have represented England while playing for Coventry: keeper Reg Mathews, 1956; defender Danny Thomas, 1983; striker Cyrille Regis, 1987 and striker Dion Dublin, 1998.

3 times Coventry City have finished a season as league champions: Division Three (South), 1935/36; Division Three, 1963/64 and Division Two, 1966/67.

1 major trophy, so far, is all City have to show for their 128 years of football history – the magical FA Cup win of 1987.

SKY BLUE SONG

After arriving at Highfield Road in late 1961, Jimmy Hill soon set about changing the club from top to bottom. As part of his rebranding mission he decided the fans needed a new anthem to sing and between Hill and director John Camkin, a reworking of the 'Eton Boating Song' came about.

Hopefully, it will not be too long before the Sky Blue song will reverberate around the top flight once again. It is interesting though to see how Jimmy Hill's original lyrics were altered, out went The Oysters and in came Chelsea, as City progressed up the leagues under Hill's own inspired stewardship in the 1960s.

Original:	Current:
Let's all sing together	Lets all sing together
Play up, Sky Blues	Play up, Sky Blues
While we sing together	While we sing together
We will never lose	We will never lose
Proud Posh or Cobblers	Tottenham or Chelsea
Oysters or anyone*	United or anyone
They shan't defeat us	They shan't defeat us
We'll fight 'til the game	We'll fight 'til the game
is won!	is won!
City! City! City!	**City! City! City!**

Of course, since dropping into the Championship, City fans have had every reason to rework the lyrics once again, but so far the allure of: 'Grimsby, Crewe, Stockport, Gillingham, Milton Keynes Dons or anyone', has been resisted!

* 'Proud Posh, Cobblers and Oysters' are, of course, Peterborough United, Northampton Town and Colchester United.

DID YOU KNOW?

The Man who Defied Time

After debuting for Chesterfield in 1977, Steve Ogrizovic continued to play professionally until 2000. Sixteen of his twenty-three seasons were spent on duty at Highfield Road and this longevity marks him out as one of only four players to have ever played top-flight football in four different decades. Peter Shilton, John Lukic and Sir Stanley Matthews are the other long-standing servants of the game, keeping Oggy company in a very select group.

The Also-Rans

Statistically, the Sky Blues are arguably the least successful English side of the last 40 years. Not since 1970, when they achieved sixth spot in the old First Division have City finished in the top six of any division, no other English league side has waited so long for a top-six finishing position. Of course, statistics never tell the whole story and City did enjoy three decades of top-flight fare, with a Wembley win thrown in for good measure. However, City fans under the age of 50 would probably struggle to remember such a high league position and are crying out for a league season to savour!

Skin of the Teeth

In Coventry's thirty-four consecutive years of top-flight football, it is fair to say they gained a reputation for contriving impossible-looking, last-minute escapes from relegation. Like a latter-day Harry Houdini, the Sky Blues repeatedly stared almost certain disaster in the face, before somehow wriggling their way to safety yet again.

Although the chains of relegation finally did shackle the Sky Blues in 2001, it is astonishing to think that they had previously survived ten last-match-of-the-season scares. On any one of those occasions, had the Sky Blues and others not secured the right combination of results, their ship would have sunk. Sadly, the old line trotted out by Ron Atkinson that, 'if the *Titanic* had been sky blue, it would never have gone down' eventually did run aground at Villa Park in 2001, but for all those years beforehand, it was quite a ride!

CITY'S BEST FA CUP RUNS – PART II

1962/63

Round 1	(H)	B'mouth & Boscombe Ath	1–0
Round 2	(A)	Millwall	0–0
Round 2 (r)	(H)	Millwall	2–1
Round 3	(A)	Lincoln City	5–1
Round 4	(A)	Portsmouth	1–1
Round 4 (r)	(H)	Portsmouth	2–2
Round 4 (r2)	(N)	Portsmouth	2–1
Round 5	(H)	Sunderland	2–1
Quarter-final	(H)	Manchester United	1–3

This first season under Jimmy Hill's stewardship marked a turning point in City's history; Hill's infectious energy, enthusiasm and sheer football knowledge was beginning to make its mark. The days of Third Division mediocrity were finishing as City finished in fourth place in the league and enjoyed a spectacular run to the FA Cup quarter-finals.

The run began in low-key fashion with home wins over Third Division rivals Bournemouth and Millwall. Fourth Division strugglers Lincoln City were up next, but the dreadful winter of that year ensured that fans had a very long wait; it was finally played nearly 2 months later, after no less than fifteen postponements! Second Division Portsmouth proved tougher opponents as they took City to a second replay, decided at White Hart Lane.

Promotion-chasing Sunderland of the Second Division came next and due to the backlog of matches caused by the harshest winter for decades, both teams knew the prize that was at stake – a home quarter-final against Matt Busby's Manchester United. Reports at the time suggest the official crowd of 40,487 was plain wrong;

turnstiles shut early, fans entered without paying and others watched from the floodlights, the roof of the stand and the edge of the pitch. Whatever the actual attendance that night, Highfield Road had not seen a crowd like this for 30 years, and never before had such a glamourous prize been on offer.

The match lived up to all expectations as a fantastic cup tie was played out. All the ingredients for a classic were present; City were the lower-league underdogs aiming to topple Sunderland, their more illustrious opponents; a floodlit Highfield Road was overflowing with fans desperate for their first cup success in over 50 years and the game itself contained a dramatic comeback.

Sunderland led early and despite City's pressure, kept their narrow advantage until the last 10 minutes. When Dietmar Bruck's shot, or perhaps cross, bounced in off a post, City fans could not contain their excitement and the first of three pitch invasions began. The second encroachment followed just minutes later after the winning goal was headed in by captain George Curtis. The 'Iron Man' powered home a cross from full-back John Sillett, in an early working of the combination that would bring City future FA Cup glories. At the final whistle as the stadium erupted and some fans made their third visit of the night onto the pitch, there was a sense that Jimmy Hill's Coventry were not just talking a good game, they were, at last, playing one too.

The quarter-final against United was just days away and to avoid the crowd chaos of the Sunderland tie, the club declared the match all-ticket. This led to thousands and thousands queueing in the rain throughout a miserable, wet Wednesday. All home tickets were sold out within hours, guaranteeing another bumper crowd.

Though quarter-final opponents Manchester United were still rebuilding from the dark days of the Munich air disaster just 5 years earlier, with Law, Charlton and Crerand in their ranks, Busby's team were beginning to stir; City were massive underdogs once again. Within 5 minutes City's Terry Bly had scored and before 20 minutes were on the clock, City nearly did it again, hitting a post. Sadly though, that was about as good as things were to get for City, as Bobby Charlton equalised before the half-hour, before putting United ahead just after the break. City pressed and pressed and did come close to levelling things up, hitting the woodwork and seeing a goal disallowed, but it was to no avail as United went on to score a third decisive goal through Albert Quixall.

While defeat signalled the end of a twenty-two-match unbeaten run, there was still much for Coventry fans to be optimistic about; the team were still challenging for promotion and the days of being Division Three also-rans were, at last, fast disappearing.

THE MAGNIFICENT SEVEN

As City ended 1997, another campaign of struggle seemed to be unfolding. A Boxing Day defeat at West Ham saw the Sky Blues slip to seventeenth and with midfield mainstay Gary McAllister now missing with a long-term injury, the storm clouds were gathering.

If ever a season could be said to have had a turning point though, it was surely that 1997/98 one. With just five minutes remaining of their next match, City trailed league leaders Manchester United 2–1 and the Christmas cheer was disappearing fast out of Highfield Road.

When David Burrows's throw found Darren Huckerby halfway down the United right flank, he was surrounded by two defenders and there seemed little danger.

Huckerby did what he often did best, he just ran simply and directly at the defenders. He first toyed with John Curtis before skipping past Henning Berg and it was then the Norwegian stopper stuck out a leg and conceded a penalty. When Dion Dublin calmly dispatched the spot-kick City looked set for a morale-boosting point against the defending champions. Huckerby, though, had other ideas, and moments later he collected the ball in similar no-man's land, this time on United's left side. After twisting and turning through half of the United team, Huckerby tiptoed into the penalty area and, like a golfer making his putt, he expertly rolled the ball home for a Christmas present to remember.

Just days later, Huckerby, and a newly energised City were at it again as they went to Anfield and humbled Liverpool 3–1 in the FA Cup. Another solo strike from Huckerby set the tone for a magnificent team effort and it signalled the start of a special time for City fans. For the next month, City simply roared on, winning seven straight matches, five in the league and two in the FA Cup, to establish a new club record.

This spell probably represented the pinnacle for several of the City squad in their time at Coventry. New arrival George Boateng added ballast to an already competitive midfield usually made up of Trond Soltvedt, Noel Whelan and Paul Telfer. The settled defence often included Dion Dublin partnering Gary Breen, in front of the emerging and impressive Magnus Hedman. On top of all of that, Darren Huckerby arguably played the best football of his City career that springtime, tormenting defenders up and down the Premiership.

They were heady days indeed, however without the intervention of Henning Berg's leg, there may never have been an equaliser against United, or super strikes from Huckerby against both United and Liverpool. That, of course, is speculation, but what remains irrefutable fact is that not so very long ago, City took on, and beat, all-comers for seven magnificent matches.

24/1/98	Derby County	(home FA Cup R4)	2–0
31/1/98	Bolton	(away)	5–1
7/2/98	Sheffield Wed	(home)	1–0
14/2/98	Aston Villa	(away FA Cup R5)	1–0
18/2/98	Southampton	(away)	2–1
21/2/98	Barnsley	(home)	1–0
28/2/98	Crystal Palace	(away)	3–0

DOUBLE-ACTS –
WALLACE & FERGUSON

For a time, in the late 1970s, the Sky Blues fielded not just one, but two goalscoring strikers whom other teams often cast envious glances at. In a classic big man–little man combination, a darting ball of red hair called Ian Wallace was partnered by the less mobile, more ponderous Mick Ferguson, a bear of a man. As can happen with contrasting players though, the opposites began to chime and the duo went on to lead many defences a merry dance.

Ferguson had been picked up by the Sky Blues as a promising youth player and patiently made his way through the ranks, debuting in 1975. Towering over defenders and possessing a terrific ability to time a header, Ferguson clearly had potential. If the young target-man was to graduate to first-team regular though, what he, and City needed, was a striker to feed off the aerial scraps he could provide. Within 18 months of Ferguson's debut a little known Scot arrived from Dumbarton; Ian Wallace may have learnt his trade at Dumbarton's

Boghead Park, but there was to be nothing bog-standard about his Coventry career.

The 1976/77 season at Highfield Road will always be best remembered for its last few minutes, when the Sky Blues and Bristol City contrived a relegation escape. However, it was also the year that the seeds of the Wallace and Ferguson partnership were planted. After a stop-start beginning to the year, courtesy of Wallace's serious car crash, the pair finished the season strongly, scoring 13 times in 18 matches, including a Wallace hat-trick against Peter Shilton's Stoke. After the relegation dust clouds finally settled there was plenty for City fans to look forward to the following year; Wallace was quick and knew how to finish; Ferguson knew how to finish, and how to assist – the portents were good.

City's 1977/78 campaign was terrific; in their 34-year tenure in the top flight that seventh-placed finish was bettered only once, while the return of 75 league goals never was. Had Ipswich not defeated Arsenal in the 1978 FA Cup final, City would even have been rewarded for their efforts with European football the next season, dizzy heights indeed.

Gordon Milne placed the emphasis on bold, attacking play, and he had the players to make it work. A midfield bolstered by the tigerish Terry Yorath, boosted by ever-present Barry Powell and ably assisted by the peerless Tommy Hutchison provided City's two strikers with plenty of chances. While Ferguson was towering and dominant in the air, Wallace was like a newly lit firework, fizzing with energy and ready to explode in the penalty area. Wallace and Ferguson flourished, notching 40 goals between them.

Ferguson's best days at City were in that 1977/78 season. Three hat-tricks, against Man City, Wolves and Birmingham, among his 17 strikes that year marked the big man down as more than just a formidable aerial presence, he could also deliver the most precious of commodities for a striker – goals. He never lost that knack either, Ferguson was not far off averaging a goal every two starts for City throughout his time at the club, despite struggling for fitness. In the next three seasons he played less than 50 times, and by the time he secured a move to Everton in August 1981, he was spending more time battling injuries than centre-halves.

At his peak, Wallace had caught people's eyes for more than just his ginger perm; he was fleet of foot, quick to shoot and capable of moments of brilliance – his bicycle kick in the 5–4 Christmas win over Norwich that year was sensational. The little man soon established a big reputation for finishing and the Coventry striker was widely coveted. Wallace played like his life depended on it; his energy and determination to get to the ball before any defender stood out almost as much as his mop of hair. The regular goals, with some spectacular strikes on the way, made Wallace a star and at his best he lit up Highfield Road better than the old floodlights.

Although the pair remained at Highfield Road for a further two years, their outings together were limited and the heights that the team hit in the 1977/78 campaign were not to be scaled again. Further individual highlights for the strikers did follow though. Ferguson's 4-goal show against Ipswich, was celebrated in the memorable 'Ferguson 4 Ipswich 1' scoreboard display and in a 1984 loan spell he returned to hit 3 vital goals in a successful relegation escape. Wallace went on to achieve international recognition for Scotland and in his last 2 years at City he became more and more highly regarded. After being a regular goalscorer for three full seasons, Wallace finally left to join the European Cup holders, Nottingham Forest, for a then mouth-watering fee of £1.25 million.

Sadly for City fans, the devastating partnership Wallace and Ferguson forged became as short-lived as it had been effective. For a little less than a whole season (Ferguson missed a dozen league games that year), the pairing had worked perfectly; the team was winning; the goals were flowing and the duo were deadly. Wallace and Ferguson may not have lasted for long, but the thrilling memories they gave to City fans in the autumn of 1977 and the spring of 1978, will last a footballing lifetime.

SKY BLUE CULTURE

City's only FA Cup final so far resulted in an obligatory Cup final song; the much-loved 'Go For It City'. The song was more of a local than a national hit, peaking only at 61 in the official charts, but it did reverberate around Highfield Road on many occasions. The memorable lyrics were usually edited to a quick burst of the chorus, but for those in the mood for a little nostalgia, key lines included:

> City's marching on
> Led by George and John
> It's gonna be our day
> When we walk down Wembley Way
>
> Killer lurks about
> Oggy keeps them out
> Sky Blues shooting to win
> Go for it, go for it City
> Sky Blues shooting to win

Interestingly, the enthusiasm for cup final records that year reached as far as Albert Square, Walford. The week after the 1987 final, the Spurs cup final ditty, 'Hot-Shot Tottenham', could be heard in the background of an *Eastenders* episode; the hopeful producers were in no way demonstrating a southern bias of course!

While the Sky Blues have played host to countless dramas over the years, strangely enough, once or twice the dramas have come to the football club and filmed themselves.

In 2005, the TV detective show *Dalziel & Pascoe* used the Highfield Road stadium to film part of an episode concerning fictional Weatherton Wanderers, while hard-hitting, cockney actor Ray Winstone braved the Ricoh Arena to film scenes as a Premiership manager for Channel Four's football drama *All in the Game*.

SPONSORS

By the late 1970s the FA had agreed to follow the European clubs' example and allow sides to display sponsorship on their shirts. Take-up was slow initially, as both BBC and ITV refused to show games featuring sponsored shirts.

City tried to work a way around the blanket ban on shirt advertising by launching their famous Talbot 'T' shirt in 1981. The Talbot logo was a fundamental part of the shirt's design, but it was not enough to satisfy the TV companies of the time, who boycotted the Sky Blues until they introduced an alternative strip for televised games.

In those early corporate days at one point there was even talk of City changing their name to accommodate their sponsors; Coventry City could conceivably have become Coventry Talbot. Bearing in mind the frequency with which teams can change their sponsorship deals, it was probably a good thing CCFC remained the name on the badge.

Finally, in 1983, the impasse was broken and TV companies relented; this allowed sponsorship deals to become the major source of revenue to clubs which they still are to this day.

Coventry City Shirt Sponsors

1981–3	Talbot Cars
1983–4	Tallon Pens
1984–5	Glazepta
1985–6	Elliotts
1986–8	Granada Bingo
1989–97	Peugeot
1998–2005	Subaru
2005–10	Cassidy Group
2010–11	City Link

THE ENTERTAINERS – PETER NDLOVU

Peter Ndlovu split opinions like he sometimes split opposing defences – right down the middle. Some people say that Ndlovu promised more than he delivered for City, and to a point that may be true, but it is worth remembering though, that the promise he offered was rarely seen at Highfield Road. Derided for his inconsistencies, Ndlovu's 39 top-flight strikes in six seasons bear testament to the wide man's enduring worth.

When Peter Ndlovu was on song his slight, sinewy figure would dribble, run and shoot all in an instant. He could collect the ball on the left flank, feign to move one way before going the other; leaving a flat-footed full-back in his wake. Ndlovu was different; speedy, irritating and full of venom, he darted at defenders like a wasp darts at its prey.

The highlight of Ndlovu's first season was scoring the only goal against Aston Villa. Receiving the ball 40 yards out and surrounded by Villa shirts, he took the ball in his stride and moved it from one foot to another at mesmerising speed; Ndlovu's jiving hips toyed with his opponents, before mercilessly firing home. The man with the tricky name now demanded attention; Nuddy had arrived.

The following season, as City flickered briefly under the guidance of Bobby Gould, Ndlovu was beginning to cause havoc up and down the country; leaving defenders trailing, commentators tongue-tied and City fans gasping for more.

Match of the Day cameras captured his dazzling footwork against early table-toppers Norwich City. Ndlovu's goal that day included more dummies than the average branch of Mothercare, and he was fast becoming a hot property. At that time Ndluvo seemed to be the answer to the City fans' prayers; he was quick, skillful and scoring great goals, all he had to do was keep it up.

Unfortunately, as City endured successive seasons of struggle under Gould, Neal and then Atkinson, Ndlovu's star began to shine only intermittently. His moments of sublime skill were becoming occasional treats, rather than the once-threatened norm.

Of all the Ndlovu highlights, perhaps the most fondly remembered might be a night of high jinks at Anfield in 1995. The match was a cracker, with City storming to a thoroughly deserved 3–2 victory; the memorable night saw Ndlovu produce a startling performance of pace, skill and goals – 3 of them. After belting in a right wing cross and converting a penalty in the first half, Ndlovu had to bide his time for his hat-trick opportunity.

A rare misplaced pass from Jan Molby gave Nuddy the ball in midfield. He ran directly at an alarmed Liverpool defence. Neil Ruddock was right to be worried, for it was as if Ndlovu had chosen him as his dancing partner, but had forgotten to tell him which tune was to be played. While Ndlovu shimmied to the left; Ruddock shifted to the right; while Ndlovu tiptoed to the right, 'Razor' slid to the left. When Ndlovu buried his shot into the Kop goal he became the first visiting player to score a hat-trick at Anfield for over 30 years, and it was then that his name shone brightest.

Though Ndlovu continued to dance his way across the flanks, his brilliance dimmed as injuries took a toll. Long-term doubts over his troublesome knee finally brought down the curtain on Ndlovu's 7-year Highfield Road career. Like a shooting star, he had fizzed and dazzled in equal measure, but like a shooting star, he was destined not to last.

CITY SUPREMOS

Historically, Coventry City have always done their bit for the unemployment figures of the nation by regularly changing their man in the hot seat. In the 60 years since the end of the Second World War, City have employed over thirty first-team managers:

Dick Bayliss	1945–7
Billy Frith	1947–8
Harry Storer	1948–53
Jack Fairbrother	1953–4
Charlie Elliott	1954–5
Jesse Carver	1955–6
George Raynor	1956

Harry Warren	1956–7
Billy Frith	1957–61
Jimmy Hill	1961–7
Noel Cantwell	1967–72
Joe Mercer	1972–4
Gordon Milne	1974–81
Dave Sexton	1981–3
Bobby Gould	1983–4
Don Mackay	1984–6
George Curtis	1986–7
John Sillett	1987–90
Terry Butcher	1990–2
Don Howe	1992
Bobby Gould	1992–3
Phil Neal	1993–5
Ron Atkinson	1995–6
Gordon Strachan	1996–2001
Roland Nilsson	2001–2
Gary McAllister	2002–3
Eric Black	2003–4
Peter Reid	2004–5
Micky Adams	2005–7
Iain Dowie	2007–8
Chris Coleman	2008–10
Aidy Boothroyd	2010–11
Andy Thorn	2011–

There have several short-term, temporary appointments as well in between permanent mangers. In the same period, it is a little depressing to note that the most successful post-war English clubs, Manchester United and Liverpool, have employed only seven and twelve full-time managers respectively.

DID YOU KNOW?

The Striker Who Couldn't Score
In the autumn of 1989, the £800,000 City spent on then-record signing Kevin Drinkell seemed to be a smart piece of business. Drinkell scored in each of his first three matches and he looked to be just what the Sky Blues needed – a more than handy top-flight scorer. Sadly, Drinkell peaked early in his City career; when he scored against Nottingham Forest the following March no-one realised that he was about to embark on a scoring drought of near biblical proportions. In two further years service at Highfield Road, the record-breaking star striker scored . . . no further goals.

The Sky Blues' International Man of Mystery
Just three years after retiring from the professional ranks, Steve Ogrizovic was reported to have been taken prisoner by the Kazakhstan government. Reports centered on Oggy having inadvertently strayed into a top-secret Kazakhstan military zone in the course of a fund-raising walk for a UK-based charity for young goalkeepers.

Fears that Oggy was to be charged with being a spy quickly took hold and in response an online petition was started to demand the return of the record-breaking keeper. Happily, the story died immediately when Oggy was able to give an interview with the *Coventry Evening Telegraph*, reassuring everyone that he was far from the confines of a Kazakh cell, and was, in fact, working with the reserves at Ryton!

Top to Bottom
Coventry City is the only team in England to have played in each of the seven divisions of the Football League. Due to a geographical reorganisation of the leagues

in the 1920s, City went from competing in Division Three North in 1925/26, to Division Three South the following year. Although it can be tempting to look at the comparative lack of achievement that City have enjoyed, it might be worth remembering that they have only spent one season in the bottom rung of the League – the 1958/59 campaign which saw City promoted at the first time of asking form Division Four, a place to which they have not yet returned!

The seven divisions consist of: Divisions One to Four, Division Three (South and North), plus the Premier League. Of the seven different tables that City have stood in, so far, they have only ever been champions on three occasions – Division Three South 1935/36, Division Three 1963/64 and Division Two 1966/67.

EVENING ALL

Interestingly enough while the Sky Blues spent many years patrolling the top flight of English football, the footballing need for discipline, for laws and for order clearly rubbed off on some City stars who went on to turn out for some very different Boys in Blue!

Ex-1970s winger Don Nardiello swapped his shift on the Highfield Road wing to pound the beat in a new career as a police officer. Nardiello had enjoyed some sparkling moments in Sky Blue, particularly during the 1978/79 season, but after returning from America's NASL without a club, he faced an uncertain future. He opted for the security of the Boys in Blue, even completing his initial training in Ryton, near his old City training ground!

At the end of a long and successful pro career, cup-winner Greg Downs, also found his way to the uniformed ranks when he signed on as a policeman in Norfolk. For some time, he combined paying non-league with his new day job; Downs turned out for several non-league clubs and played well into his 40s. Hopefully, the many years of tracking down opposing wingers, would have served Downs well in his future career, tracking down fleeing felons.

City stopper Steve Ogrizovic famously pulled on the Sky Blue keeper's jersey on 601 occasions; however stopping villians, not shots, was his first career choice. The young Oggy signed up for the Police Force, and had he not been spotted by Chesterfield, it might have been a career of thwarting top-flight villains rather than top-flight strikers.

The Boys in Blue theme has recently been revived through the unlikely figure of Dutch defender Arjan de Zeeuw. Brought in by Iain Dowie to add defensive know-how to a hoped-for promotion push, things never worked out for the burly defender. Injuries and some erratic form led to de Zeeuw playing less than 20 games for City and just a year later he had retired from the game to take up a position with his local Dutch police force as an investigative detective. The mystery of why City drafted in an aging, slowing, burly defender might well be one that has to sit in de Zeeuw's intray as unresolved.

CITY'S BEST LEAGUE CUP RUNS – PART II

1980/81

Round 2, L1	(A)	Manchester United	1–0
Round 2, L2	(H)	Manchester United	1–0
Round 3	(A)	Brighton & Hove Albion	2–1
Round 4	(H)	Cambridge United	1–1

Round 4 (r)	(A)	Cambridge United	1–0
QF	(A)	Watford	2–2
QF (r)	(H)	Watford	5–0
SF, L1	(H)	West Ham United	3–2
SF, L2	(A)	West Ham United	0–2

The run to City's first ever semi-final spot began with a double over Manchester United and was followed by lower-key victories over Brighton and then Cambridge, in a replay. The touchpaper was well and truly lit, though, when Watford came out of the hat for the quarter-final draw, as fans spotted the chance to progress into a first ever semi-final after 97 years of trying. It was comfortable in the end, but only after City had scrapped all the way to a 2–2 draw at Vicarage Road. The 5-0 replay win was witnessed by over 30,000 home fans who revelled in the fact that, at last, a major final was within touching distance.

Gordon Milne's team was full of youthful talent and in the home leg against West Ham, many of the players came of age. In one of the most thrilling matches ever seen at Highfield Road – City recovered from an early two-goal deficit to take a narrow lead to Upton Park, courtesy of goals from the indomitable Garry Thompson and midfield craftsman, Gerry Daly. Although all Sky Blue hearts were broken by a late winner from West Ham in the second leg, at that time City's future looked assured. Gary Gillespie, Paul Dyson and Danny Thomas were the young guns in defence while the attacking flair of Peter Bodak, Mark Hateley and Garry Thompson boded well for the future. Sadly, within a little over two years none of the players remained and by the time Bobby Gould took up the managerial reins, it was revolution not evolution for the next City team.

GIANTS KILLED

25 November 1961 became a red-letter day in Coventry City history for all the wrong reasons. In normal circumstances, a second round FA Cup tie at home against Southern League King's Lynn should not have presented too many problems, but on that day normal circumstances did not seem to apply. City had already produced one shocking cup performance that season, being well beaten 3–0 by Division Four Workington, a display which was so poor that, at the time, it was considered one of the club's worst ever. In that respect at least, City had form, just not the form the fans wanted.

City began the match poorly; King's Lynn had more possession and looked more likely to do something with it, while City were sluggish. Strangely, though, when the opening goal came after almost half an hour, it fell to City, courtesy of a King's Lynn own goal after Peter Hill had threatened down the right. What should have been a tonic to City seemed more of an upset, as they contrived to concede twice before half time, with goals from Johnson and Wright. One of the grimmest intervals ever seen at Highfield Road passed in sombre mood, with the home fans incredulous at what they had just witnessed.

In the second period City attacked with fear and anxiety more prominent than any players, yet still they almost rescued a dire situation, twice going close to an equaliser. It was, however, King's Lynn's day and the Southern Leaguers fully deserved their place in the third round. For City, this result was probably their worst ever; chairman of the time, Derrick Robins, declared it, 'utterly disastrous' and few could argue. Within days the management team was sacked and a new face came to steer the Coventry City ship, one Jimmy Hill.

PACKING THEM IN

Since the Sky Blue era began in the summer of 1962, attendances have ebbed and flowed like the team itself. Here are some of the ups and downs:

Highest Attendances at Highfield Road

51,452	Division 2	(3–1)	Wolves	29/4/1967
47,111	Division 1	(2–0)	Man Utd	16/3/1968
45,402	Division 1	(2–1)	Man Utd	8/4/1969

Highest Attendances at Highfield Road (after it went all-seater)

27,509	Division 1	(1–4)	Liverpool	29/8/1987
26,657	Division 1	(1–0)	Liverpool	2/5/1987
24,410	Prem	(0–1)	Man Utd	12/4/1993

Lowest Attendances at Highfield Road(*)

7,478	Division 1	(0–2)	Watford	18/1/1986
8,035	Division 1	(2–0)	Brighton	4/12/1983
8,294	Division 1	(0–1)	Wimbledon	16/12/1989

Highest Attendances at The Ricoh Arena (**)

31,407	FA Cup R6	(0–2)	Chelsea	7/3/2009
28,184	Cham	(2–3)	Leeds United	6/11/2010
28,163	FA Cup R5	(0–5)	WBA	16/2/2008

Lowest Attendances at The Ricoh Arena

12,292	Cham	(2–1)	Doncaster R	28/9/2010
13,169	Cham	(2–1)	Derby County	21/8/2010
14,036	Cham	(1–1)	Scunthorpe Utd	24/11/2007

The time in City's history when they were best supported, not surprisingly, coincided with their promotion to Division One in 1967. The first three seasons in Division

One all attracted average home gates of 30,000+, peaking at an average of 34,705 in 1967/68. The single highest gate was, and will remain, the Wolves game from 1967. Dubbed 'The Midlands Match of the Century' at the time, the championship decider of 1967 was a unique occasion for all City fans, as the Sky Blues sat on the cusp of top-flight football for the first time.

After the stadium became an all-seater in 1981 when the capacity was much reduced, City's best supported season was 1999/2000. It was the year that Gordon Strachan's team did not win a single away match, but did win many plaudits for their home performances. Inspired by McAllister, Hadji and Keane, Gordon Strachan's 'Team of Entertainers' averaged 20,786 a game as they provided fans with some memorable matches.

* City did play a Full Members' Cup tie against Millwall in the autumn of 1986, which officially attracted 1,086 supporters through the turnstiles. The competition was short-lived, due to the rise of the Premier League, and the limited enthusiasm of the supporters!

** The Ricoh has twice attratcted 30,000+ crowds for other fixtures involving the England U21 team, and also for a rugby union Heineken Cup tie.

DOUBLE-ACTS –
BRIAN KILCLINE & TREVOR PEAKE

Trevor Peake joined City in the summer of 1983 at the relatively late age of 26, having come up the football ladder through both non-league and the lower divisions. In his first season Peake was partnered at the heart of the City defence by the experienced figure of Sam Allardyce.

That first year set the tone for the following seasons; after an erratic campaign with City only scrambling to safety on the last day of the season. Peake had impressed in his debut season with solid tackling and smart positional play throughout; his future as a top-flight defender looked assured, but with Allardyce departing, he needed a new centre-back partner.

The summer of 1984 brought just what Peake and City needed in the shape of Brian Kilcline. Physically, Kilcline was a beast of a man; he was an imposing figure, standing well over 6ft, and with plenty of weight to throw around. City were then able to field a contrasting pairing in central defence. Though Kilcline did not lack in football intelligence, his speciality was the brawn; always on the lookout for the next forward to demolish. Peake was almost his polar opposite; able to mix it physically, but his forte lay in reading the game and being in the right place at the right time.

With Kilcline and Peake, it might have been a case of the sum total of the players being worth more than they were individually. Though Peake was often regarded as being close to international class – he missed out through injury on representing England B in 1987 – not many people pushed the international claims of Brian Kilcline. As the pairing were reliable and solid, rather than outstanding, and because they played so long beside each other, perhaps they were viewed more as part of a pair than individuals in their own right. The fact that both could play a little should not be underestimated.

Kilcline tackled like a JCB digger and though some fans thought he was not much quicker than one either, he had a big, burly presence that few opposing forwards relished facing. Not many City players have ever hit a dead ball with the velocity of Kilcline; once he hit a ball it stayed hit! His free-kicks and penalties also brought him a handy goals return for a defender. His goal, minutes from time, of a match City had to win against Luton in May 1985, proved vital. His thumping low drive secured a narrow win, when 5 more goalless minutes would have meant City being relegated and the FA Cup winners of 1987 would never have stayed together.

Peake was never an agricultural defender like Kilcline; his game did not involve the indiscriminate scything down of anyone. Not blessed with lightning pace, Peake compensated for that by seeing things early and acting accordingly. He had an excellent sense of how to play different strikers, deep one week, higher up the pitch the next. His tactical intelligence and well-timed tackles meant Peake was seldom left for dead by forwards who may have been quicker over 20 yards, but were never quicker-witted. For defensive know-how, he wrote the manual.

The double-act of Kilcline and Peake stood tall and firm for some relatively prosperous top-flight years, as well as, with Steve Ogrizovic, being the rock on which the FA Cup-winning team was built on. Their defensive partnership provided a cornerstone for the team for years. Their nicely contrasting qualities gelled like few defensive pairings have before or since; Peake provided the polish to Kilcline's rough edges and between them they shone brightly.

CITY IN EUROPE

After achieving their highest ever top-flight finish of sixth in the 1969/70 season, the Sky Blues qualified for European football the following season. City entered the European Fairs Cup, the forerunner of the UEFA Cup, and started impressively with two victories over Bulgaria's Trakia Plovdiv. A John O'Rourke hat-trick in

THE COVENTRY CITY MISCELLANY

a 4–1 win in Plovdiv, watched by fewer than 40 away fans, made the home leg a relaxed affair with a 2–1 success following. However, City's European adventure ended in abrupt fashion in the next round at the hands of German powerhouses Bayern Munich.

Munich's line-up included some fantastic figures from German football of the 1960s and '70s: goalkeeping great Sepp Maier, legendary libero Franz Beckenbauer and then European Footballer of the Year and 1970 World Cup top scorer Gerd Müller. For City to have got past that team would have been a remarkable feat, but Bayern were just too strong. A 6–1 thumping in the rain of Munich was followed by a 2–1 consolation victory at Highfield Road in the return leg. Although Munich exited to Liverpool at the quarter-final stage of the competition that year, within two years they were European Cup winners and remained so for three years running.

As time-served City fans know, that first foray into European football remains the club's only Continental competition so far. In 1978, the Wallace and Ferguson inspired team missed out on UEFA Cup qualification by just one league place, and famously the 1987 FA Cup winners were denied entry into the Cup Winners' Cup because of the post-Heysel ban on all British teams.

European Fairs Cup 1970/71
1st Round

Away	Trakia Plovdiv (Bulgaria)	Won 4–1
Home	Trakia Plovdiv (Bulgaria)	Won 2–0

Won 6–1 on aggregate

2nd Round

Away	Bayern Munich (West Germany)	Lost 6–1
Home	Bayern Munich	Won 2–1

Lost 7–3 on aggregate

CITY LEGENDS – STEVE OGRIZOVIC

When Steve Ogrizovic signed for City in the summer of 1984 it is fair to say no-one could have imagined he would still be making first-team appearances some 16 years later, yet, incredibly he was. Before joining City, Oggy had graduated from Liverpool reserves to two seasons of cut-and-thrust Division Two football for Shrewsbury Town; he was seen as solid and promising, worth a look at in the top flight, but hardly a legend in the making.

Soon after his arrival, though, Ogrizovic started to impress; he made few mistakes; he handled the ball well, and commanded his area with confidence. Although he certainly could fling his huge frame around the six-yard box to fine effect, making spectacular saves was not necessarily Oggy's defining characteristic. What probably made him stand out most was his unerring judgement; he had an ability to make the right call, to know which crosses to go for and which to leave; at a relatively young age for a goalkeeper, he had mastered the art of being in the right position at the right time.

Oggy's early seasons coincided with desperate relegation battles and it was only after John Sillett and George Curtis took over the Highfield Road reins that the giant keeper was able to start looking up, rather than down the table. As that FA Cup final year developed, Oggy began to look more and more like a complete goalkeeper. He patrolled his penalty area with authority, apprehending forwards the way he was trained to apprehend felons in the police training of his youth.

Of all the fine games he played in the Wembley year, most fans would remember his saves in the semi-final against Leeds United. City started nervously, and had Oggy to thank for only trailing by a single strike at half time, diving blocks and point-blank stops particularly live in the memory. As the drama unfolded and City eventually clawed their way back into a winning position, it was Ogrizovic who again stood firm to deny Leeds a late equaliser, diving courageously at the feet of Keith Edwards to ensure City's passage to the twin towers.

After picking up the only winners' medal of his City career in the final against Spurs, Oggy continued to thrive in the top flight. His consistency, reliability and efficiency enabled him to compile a club record 209 consecutive league appearances, from August 1984 to September 1989, and he was often cited as one of the best uncapped keepers England have produced.

For a full decade after his Wembley heroics, Oggy continued to call the number one shirt his own, remaining first choice until past his 40th birthday. Indeed, it was in his last full season as first choice, 1996/97, that Oggy produced one more startling display which left City fans steeped in his debt. After a faltering season under first Ron Atkinson and then Gordon Strachan, City played their last match at Tottenham needing to beat a handy Spurs team and for other results to go their way; it looked the longest of long shots.

However, Lady Luck turned up and ensured both Middlesbrough and Sunderland failed to get what they needed and all City had to do was maintain a narrow 2–1 advantage. It was then that Ogrizovic had perhaps his finest minutes in Sky Blue as in quick succession he stopped goalbound efforts from Jason Dozzell and then Neale Fenn. In the days of inflated Premiership finances, never before had a block of Oggy's giant-sized legs been so valuable to his team. On *Match of the Day* that night, Alan Hansen suggested each save was worth £10 million to the club as had either strike gone in City would have been relegated and financially stricken. Sadly, that doomsday scenario did come to pass just 4 years later, but it is surely no coincidence that City's relegation did not occur on Oggy's watch.

After 601 first-team matches stretching over sixteen seasons, Ogrizovic's departure from the first team left a massive hole for other keepers to come along and try to fill. His enduring loyalty to the club, his presence in the goal, and his sustained excellence, place him firmly at the head of a distinguished list of City keepers.

At his best it seemed like the only thing Oggy couldn't stop was the slow march of Father Time, although by bowing out of first-team action at the age of 42 he did his best to defy him too. Oggy was as solid as the goalframes he patrolled, as unfashionable as the Sky Blue teams he represented, but almost as enduring as the Three Spires of Coventry themselves; truly, a giant of a goalkeeper.

CITY'S BEST FA CUP RUNS – PART III

1972/73

Round 3	(A)	Leyton Orient	4–1
Round 4	(H)	Grimsby Town	1–0
Round 5	(H)	Hull City	3–0
Quarter-final	(A)	Wolves	0–2

For just the third time in the club's 90-year history, City reached the FA Cup quarter-finals. Straightforward wins over Second Division Orient and Hull came either side of a narrow home win against Third Division Grimsby. That fourth round game saw a crowd of almost 40,000 witness a tough encounter which was only settled 4 minutes from time by Mick Coop's late penalty.

By the time City arrived at Molineux for the quarter-final against high-flying Wolves, thoughts were just beginning to turn towards a first outing to Wembley's twin towers. However, the experience Wolves had gained from their run to the previous year's UEFA Cup final was vital, as City wilted in front of 50,000 fans, losing 2–0. Dreams of Wembley were put on hold.

1981/82

Round 3	(H)	Sheffield Wed	3–1
Round 4	(A)	Manchester City	3–1
Round 5	(H)	Oxford United	4–0
Quarter-final	(A)	WBA	0–2

Just a year after coming so close to a first major final in the League Cup, City were threatening to reach Wembley again, this time in the FA Cup. A comfortable third round win over Sheffield Wednesday set up an intriguing rematch with former Sky Blue hero, Tommy Hutchison, who was now a fixture for Man City.

Dave Sexton's young team went to Maine Road and played superbly; the Sky Blues (decked out in a distinctive red change strip) were leading 2–0 through goals from Hunt and Hateley before a Kevin Bond penalty halved their lead. The last 15 minutes then saw an increasingly desperate Man City apply plenty of pressure, and it was from another home attack that the Sky Blues sealed their win. Peter Bodak picked the ball up 20 yards short of his own halfway line and simply galloped away with it, until he reached the edge of the Man City penalty area where he was met by the enormous frame of Joe Corrigan coming to greet him. Like a golfer in a tight spot in a bunker, Bodak expertly managed to chip the ball towards its target, and with a perfect flight it looped over Corrigan before nestling in the net. That strike won Goal of the Month and Sexton's youthful outfit were again beginning to turn heads.

A 4–0 win over Third Division Oxford in the fifth round set up an away quarter-final with a West Brom team who were no longer displaying the swagger of their previous years under Ron Atkinson. A first FA Cup semi-final seemed within City's grasp until the game began; West Brom just had too much in all areas and City suffered a 2–0 reverse. Chief architect of West Brom's performance that day, and scorer of a superb strike was Cyrille Regis, who 5 years later, was destined to play a very different part in a Coventry City FA Cup run.

SPECIAL DELIVERY SERVICE

At one point in the early 1990s, City could credibly lay claim to having the quickest striker in the country on their books. Ex-postman and promising Swansea City striker John Williams had enjoyed a decent first season for the Swans, but it was not his 11 strikes in the then Division Three that catapulted him to fame.

Williams had taken part in, and won, the 1992 Rumbelows Sprint Challenge before that year's showpiece League Cup Final. The nation's eyes were caught by the pacy front man, who ran the 100 metres in full football kit including boots in a mightily impressive 11.49 seconds, earning a cool £10,000 in the process.

Eagle-eyed, lower-league talent-spotter Bobby Gould took note and when he took over at Highfield Road later that year, Williams was soon on way to Coventry. Like Williams himself, City burst out of the inaugural Premier League blocks and found themselves heading the first league table of the new era. Five wins from the first seven matches made City a team of pacesetters and Williams' lung-bursting runs down the right wing were playing no small part in the early season success.

Not for the first time though, early promise faded as City, and Williams, found the season more of a marathon than a sprint. It was the year of Mick Quinn's goals and memorable 5-goal splashes against both Liverpool and Blackburn; undoubted highlights and moments of great fun for City fans. Sadly, a disappointing finale saw City slip to fifteenth, after spending most of the year in the top ten.

That gradual dimming of the brightspots was emblematic of Williams' own City career as he played less and less over the three seasons he stayed at Highfield Road. While Williams' Rumbelows-fuelled boots could scare and dazzle defenders, it is fair to say his delivery was probably more Royal Mail than David Beckham. For a time at least though, fans could enjoy seeing a City striker who, when he was on song, could scare the life out of opponents as he left them for dead.

DID YOU KNOW?

Two for the price of one
When Gordon Strachan signed promising Swedish full-back Tomas Gustafsson in 1999, hopes were high that City might just have unearthed the next Roland Nilsson. However, injuries and some erratic form put paid to those ideas, but Gustafsson still managed to leave an indelible mark with the City faithful, for non-footballing matters.

Apparently the full-back was worried about the number of people who shared his surname back home in his native Sweden and decided to do something about it. He took the drastic step of changing his name and went on to become known as Tomas Antonelius, taking the surname from a family connection. Sadly, neither incarnation put down roots in the Premier League, and 3 years and just fifteen appearances later, City released the enigmatic full-back.

CHAMPIONS – DIVISION TWO 1966/67

		P	W	D	L	F	A	Pts
1	Coventry City	42	23	13	6	74	43	59
2	Wolves	42	25	8	9	88	48	58
3	Carlisle United	42	23	6	13	71	54	52
4	Blackburn Rovers	42	19	13	10	56	46	51
5	Ipswich Town	42	17	16	9	70	54	50
6	Huddersfield Town	42	20	9	13	58	46	49
7	Crystal Palace	42	19	10	13	61	55	48
8	Millwall	42	18	9	15	49	58	45
9	Bolton Wanderers	42	14	14	14	64	58	42
10	Birmingham City	42	16	8	18	70	66	40
11	Norwich City	42	13	14	15	49	55	40
12	Hull City	42	16	7	19	77	72	39
13	Preston North End	42	16	7	19	65	67	39
14	Portsmouth	42	13	13	16	59	70	39
15	Bristol City	42	12	14	16	56	62	38
16	Plymouth Argyle	42	14	9	19	59	58	37
17	Derby County	42	12	12	18	68	72	36
18	Rotherham Utd	42	13	10	19	61	70	36
19	Charlton Athletic	42	13	9	20	49	53	35
20	Cardiff City	42	12	9	21	61	87	33
21	Northampton T	42	12	6	24	47	84	30
22	Bury	42	11	6	25	49	83	28

When the Sky Blues started the 1966/67 season there were grounds for real optimism. A third-place finish in

1966 had created momentum, the skilful scot Ian Gibson had been added from Middlesbrough and England had just won the World Cup!

Although the season started sluggishly, with some early away defeats, the nucleus of a promotion-winning team was in place. A spine of Glazier, Curtis, Gibson and Gould gave the team a solid base to build on, and as the season progressed so did City. While strong home form was maintained all year long, with seventeen wins in twenty-one matches at Highfield Road, away success was proving more elusive. In frustration, and perhaps anger too, manager Hill famously dropped Ian Gibson after an October reverse at Carlisle. The new man was not using his undoubted skills as Hill wanted him to and the manager made a clear point – you were a team player, or no player at all.

Gibson stewed for six games before being recalled with a point to prove. Scoring in a 3–2 win over Cardiff, the Scot showed Hill the craft his team had been missing, and a record-breaking unbeaten run of twenty-five games had begun. As spring arrived, City's and Wolves' campaigns gathered strength, leaving other challengers a distance behind; it seemed a straightforward race to the promotion line. By the end of April, when Blackburn dropped home points, City's first ever promotion to the First Division was secured and all that was left to decide was the matter of who went up as champions.

With three games left, Wolves visited Highfield Road and Jimmy Hill, a man with a talent for PR, declared the game to be 'The Midlands Match of the Century'. It probably was the Sky Blues' match of the century though, as for the first time ever, when City fans clanked through the old Highfield Road turnstiles, they were happy in the knowledge that the Sky Blues were about to join English football's elite.

For everyone who was there on 29 April 1967, the occasion and the match will linger long in the memory. The stadium was fuller than it ever had been and the official attendance was a club record 51,455. Supporters were crammed in with literally every vantage point taken; some fans filled the track around the pitch; some fans balanced precariously on the roof of stands; most famously of all, some fans climbed half-way up the floodlights, dangling like puppets on a string.

The game itself was as thrilling as the occasion. As City and Wolves sparred for superiority, the men from Molineux edged the first half and scored shortly before the interval, but Hill's Sky Blues were not content to limp to promotion. A second-half onslaught brought goals from Machin, Gibson and Rees, prompting delirious pitch invasions and the wildest explosions of joy in Coventry City's history.

On the final day of the season the championship was settled. Wolves gathered just one point from their last two fixtures, while City took three, and so, fittingly, the Sky Blues clinched the championship at Highfield Road on the last day of the season. At last, the big-time was beckoning.

THE ENTERTAINERS – DAVE BENNETT

Dave Bennett signed for City in the hectic summer of 1983, costing just £100,000 from Third Division Cardiff City. Bennett had made his name as a speedy forward with an eye for goal at Manchester City, and seemed to be just what the Sky Blues needed.

In an eventful first season Bennett soon impressed with his control, pace and attacking threat. City roared up to fourth by Christmas and hopes were high. However, they barely won another match all season and needed Bennett's last-match winner to secure safety. This seemed to set the tone for much of Bennett's stay at City; on occasions, usually the bigger ones, he could certainly produce the goods, typically with a smile on is face as wide as his leggy runs. Watching Bennett, his ability was never in doubt – the darting runs, the clever footwork and the odd goal all showed what he could do, but, like so many wingers, consistency was the problem.

In 1986, Bennett ended his third season at City with another crucial relegation-saving strike, against QPR, but things remained a struggle. However, the joint appointment of Sillett and Curtis that summer changed things dramatically. Bennett was finally playing in a side that allowed him to do what he did best – attack defenders while others worried about defending.

The 1986/87 season included some electrifying performances from Bennett, showing he had finally added that magical missing ingredient – consistency. Bennett's FA Cup final performance showed his full repertoire of tricks; from tiptoeing through the Spurs defence to equalise, to setting up Keith Houchen's wonder goal, he was involved in most of the good things City did.

Injuries limited Bennett's subsequent career and his stylish play was rarely seen after he left Highfield Road, but Sky Blues fans certainly saw his best days, when he danced down the wing to great effect.

COVENTRY KIDS

Over the years several Coventry-born players have gone on to play for the Sky Blues. Each one has carried more than just the usual supporters' hopes with them, with local fans relating so much more easily to their hometown heroes, there can be a burden of expectation too. Two recent players who have thrived on the distinction of playing for their home team, have been Marcus Hall and Gary McSheffrey.

Hall came up through the ranks before signing YTS forms in 1992. He swapped Stoke Park School and life at home for the Sky Blue Lodge and £29.50 a week as he started out. Within two years he was coming on as a sub for the first team and beginning to establish himself as a valuable member of the first-team squad. Hall was a solid left-back who was blessed with a sweet delivery and the ability to make a well-timed, crunching tackle. Although he was seldom spectacular he was always a dependable defender and not many wide men ever got the better of him.

After relegation from the top flight Hall moved on, but within three years he came back to shore up City's now Championship defence. Throughout his two spells, and over 300 appearances, Hall brought quality, consistency and complete commitment to the Sky Blue cause; his obvious sense of pride in representing his hometown team made him a hugely respected figure, both on and off the pitch.

Gary McSheffrey is about as local a player as it is possible to have; he was brought up on Swan Lane, adjacent to the Highfield Road stadium itself. His earliest days were spent just minutes away at St Benedict's primary school, and his footballing skills soon stood out. McSheffrey was spotted by the Sky Blues and made his way up through the academy ranks, appearing in two losing Youth Cup finals along the way.

In 1999, when McSheffrey made his first-team debut in a memorable 4–1 win at Villa Park, he became both the club and the Premier League's youngest ever player, at 16 years and 197 days. McSheffrey was a young man with a burgeoning reputation; he seemed to have rewritten the goalscoring manual for youth football and hopes were high for a top-flight career. However, before McSheffrey could begin to make an impact in the Premier League, injuries restricted his opportunities and City were relegated within two years.

After loan spells at Luton in successive years, McSheffrey began to force his way back into the side and fans found a lot to warm to; quick feet, direct running and an eye for goal marked him out. He could score from a central position or coming in from the left flank and as the goals flew in, his popularity soared. Unfortunately, as McSheffrey started making the right sort of headlines, the Sky Blues did not. Their crippling debts meant they never threatened to get close to even a play-off position and by the time Birmingham City came calling in 2006, few fans begrudged McSheffrey the chance to see if he could progress to the top flight.

McSheffrey's time at St Andrews began superbly with promotion to the top flight, but his stay was mixed, with two promotions sandwiched by a relegation season. When he agreed to rejoin City in 2010, he received the warmest of welcomes home, as fans looked forward to his characteristic darting runs and incisive finishes. Fans were not disappointed either as Goal of the Season and Supporters' Club Player of the Year awards followed in McSheffrey's first season back.

A fit and firing Gary McSheffrey is thrilling for Sky Blues fans to watch and of course he would be loved wherever he was from. This local lad from Swan Lane though, chimes with the crowds in a way few players ever do because when he scores for his team, he really does score for his City.

CHRISTMAS CRACKERS

Every year as Christmas approaches, football fans up and down the country turn out in greater than usual numbers, hoping for an extra serving of festive fun. Going back over more than 30 years here are three of City's finest Christmas crackers.

Coventry City 5–4 Norwich City
27 December 1977

If you wrote down exactly what makes a memorable match the chances are you would come up with most of what Highfield Road witnessed this December day: goals galore, twists and turns, penalties scored and saved, plus some sensational strikes – this game simply had it all. Father Christmas himself could not have left Sky Blues fans a greater present than this 9-goal thriller against Norwich.

In 1977/78 Gordon Milne's emphasis on attack was bold and resulted in one of City's brightest top-flight campaigns. The team's final place of seventh, though, seemed scant reward for their impressive 75 league goals – more than half of which were contributed by the formidable front-two of Wallace and Ferguson. In a season of great games and memories this match stood apart from every other.

City opened the scoring through an early Barry Powell penalty and doubled their lead with a sensational Ian Wallace strike. Facing away from Kevin Keelan's goal, Wallace twisted like a circus acrobat to connect with a heavenly overhead kick, leaving the 21,000 crowd gasping. These sublime heights were not maintained though and City's 2–0 advantage became a 3–2 half-time deficit as Norwich fought back.

In the second period the goals continued; Ray Gooding and Bobby McDonald nudged City back in front at 4–3, before veteran Martin Peters levelled the scores with 15 minutes left. When wide man Ray Graydon headed City 5–4 ahead once more, in the 81st minute, few spectators would have been sure that was the end of the scoring. With just a minute left Norwich were awarded a penalty, only for City keeper Jim Blyth to become a hero when he stopped John Ryan's spot-kick; the game with the Hollywood script had, for City fans, the happiest of endings.

Coventry City 4–3 Tottenham Hotspur
28 December 1986

Fast forward exactly 9 years later and a new Coventry City were emerging. The relegation-haunted team of recent seasons had taken on a very different hue under messers Sillett and Curtis; the 1986/87 side were more organised, more competitive and about to become more successful than any of their predecessors.

When Tottenham came to town at Christmas, City had played almost half a season in the top half of the league and the prospect of taking on Spurs' glittering array of internationals was nothing to fear. With both teams intent on attacking, the game ebbed and flowed for almost 40 goalless minutes. In the final 5 minutes of the first period Clive Allen scored a brace, but sandwiched in between was a towering header from the returning Keith Houchen (a sight Spurs would get to enjoy six months later at Wembley again); Spurs just about merited their 2–1 half-time advantage.

Roared on by a bumper gate of 22,000 fans, the Sky Blues came alive in a thrilling second period. Linking up superbly with frontmen Regis and Houchen, Dave Bennett twice ripped through the heart of the Spurs defence to first level, and then put the Sky Blues 3–2 ahead. Hoddle and Waddle continued to prompt and probe from a fluid midfield five, and Spurs finally replied through substitute Nico Claesen with just 5 minutes left. With the outcome in the balance, few fans headed for the exits and they were right not to.

As he had done all season, Cyrille Regis had again spearheaded most of City's attacking play that afternoon; always the focal point of the play. In the final minute, however, Regis reversed his role, from the maker to the taker of chances. He rose highest to thud the ball against Ray Clemence's crossbar, and then before anyone could react, Regis' momentum took him goalwards where he simply nodded the rebound past the grounded keeper. With a single arm aloft, Regis grinned his way past the adoring fans of the West End, having delivered a present to remember.

Coventry City 3–2 Arsenal
26 December 1999

Thanks to the Sky TV cameras, the Sky Blues were able to provide a Boxing Day feast for football fans across the country. Arsène Wenger's star-filled Arsenal arrived to face a City outfit that had started to get noticed for all the right reasons. Gordon Strachan had fashioned a team of talented players who, at least at Highfield Road, had started to click on a regular basis and even earned the nickname of 'The Entertainers'.

That year's Sky Blue vintage seemed to have a bit of everything; a touch of Moroccan magic from Hadji and Chippo; a dash of Scottish know-how and guile from leader Strachan and captain McAllister; plus a drop of Irish wit and verve from Robbie Keane's mercurial feet. On Boxing Day night, it all came together, for 90 glorious minutes.

Gary McAllister's deflected shot off Martin Keown put the Sky Blues deservedly ahead early on and before the break Mustapha Hadji added an extraordinary second goal. With Arsenal's famed defensive pillars of Adams and Keown facing him, Hadji stole half a second from somewhere, and, like an expert assassin, spotted the one vulnerable area of David Seaman's goal to aim for. Hadji's speed of thought and foot combined to loft, not blast, the ball home for a goal which in a century of football at Highfield Road might just have been unique.

As well as the quality of City's own play and goals, what made it even better for the home fans that night was the fact that their opponents were top class themselves. That Arsenal team included World Cup winners Henry and Petit, wide-man Overmars, the enigmatic Kanu as well as the usually impervious defence of Seaman, Dixon, Adams, Keown and Winterburn. To be handing them a lesson was some achievement.

The inevitable Arsenal fightback did begin after the interval and briefly gathered strength when they scored 20 minutes into the second period. Within 5 minutes, though, Robbie Keane supplied the *coup de grâce*; despite running away from goal, he applied the deftest of touches to reverse the ball back past David Seaman; a real trick-shot of a goal. Arsenal rallied and reduced their arrears to 3–2, but it was City's night and for many of the team, their own stars never shone as brightly again as on that Christmas night.

DID YOU KNOW?

The ones who got away
It is easy to be wise after any event, but City can stand accused of having let one or two outstanding talents slip through their fingers.

Future Liverpool and England star, Kevin Keegan, had trials for Jimmy Hill's Sky Blues while he was still a schoolboy. Keegan was invited back for an extended trial, but, strangely, the future European Footballer of the Year, was not rated highly enough to be offered a professional contract!

Similarly, another future England star, winger Chris Waddle, had unsuccessful trials with City when he was 16. Although his ability was clear to see, Waddle was considered too slight to go on and make the grade as a pro. He returned to the North-East very disillusioned, and instead began his working life in a sausage factory. It was almost 4 years before Waddle was able to swap skinning sausages for skinning opposition full-backs and City's loss went on to become Newcastle, Tottenham and Marseille's gain!

The ref needs glasses

When Terry Venables' much-vaunted 'Team of the Eighties' arrived to play the Sky Blues early in September 1980, the Eagles were meant to be flying high. With a bright manager, some promising players and just a little bit of luck, Palace were expected to go on and enjoy a successul season.

That day, though, Palace seemed to have forgotten to pack their fair share of Lady Luck as they became victims of one of the greatest larcenies Highfield Road ever witnessed. Trailing 2–1, the Londoners were awarded an indirect free-kick on the left-hand corner of the City penalty area. The ball was rolled to teenage striker Clive Allen who arrowed an unstoppable shot high to Jim Blyth's left. Unbelievably, when the ball bounced back onto the pitch after hitting the stanchion in the goal net, the referee refused to award the goal. After checking with both linesmen, Mr Webb insisted the ball had not crossed the line. Sadly for Palace, Allen's shot had indeed gone in, the officials all got it wrong and City got away with an outrageous piece of good fortune.

THE CUP THAT NEVER WAS

After their 1987 FA Cup triumph, the Sky Blues were denied the reward of European football due to the continuing ban on English fans imposed after the Heysel Disaster. With this outlet closed off, City instead hoped to maximise their status as FA Cup holders by setting up the Anglo-Scottish Challenge Cup against the 1987 Scottish Cup winners, St Mirren.

The Highfield Road ticket office was never overflowing with supporters queueing for tickets, but the contest may have attracted a larger crowd had the first leg not been played just 3 nights before Christmas. Prior to kick-off, both teams displayed their FA Cups to the hardy fans who had made the effort to attend – fewer than 6,000 – but the silverware on show was probably the highlight of the night as a distinctly low-key encounter finished 1–1.

Whether the pubs and offices of Coventry and Paisley were awash with talk of what might happen in the return leg at Love Street we will never know. What we do know for sure though is that 24 years later, we are still waiting for the second leg to be played!

Although problems in scheduling the second fixture and securing a sponsor for it are cited as reasons why the teams never completed their Challenge Cup decider, the underwhelming response of fans was probably part of it too. While City might just about claim to have taken part in one of the longest-running cup ties ever recorded, sadly, it seems, if you are waiting for a winner to be declared, you shouldn't hold your breath!

CITY'S BEST FA CUP RUNS – PART IV

1986/87

Round 3	(H)	Bolton Wanderers	3–0
Round 4	(A)	Manchester United	1–0
Round 5	(A)	Stoke City	1–0
QF	(A)	Sheffield Wednesday	3–1
SF	(N)	Leeds United	3–2
Final	(N)	Tottenham Hotspur	3–2

City kicked off the 1986/87 season with two men in charge of first-team affairs, ex-players John Sillett and George Curtis. Few people thought that pairing could lift City out of their years of struggle, but against expectations, the season started well. At Christmas, City were established in the top ten and were proving hard to beat, with the new-look front two of Bennett and Regis proving a handful.

On a freezing January day, City's third round FA Cup tie against Bolton was easily won. Although the match was over by half time thanks to goals from Downs, Regis and Bennett, few in the 12,000 gate would have spent too much time planning their routes to Wembley. The reward for that win was a tie at Old Trafford to take on Alex Ferguson's Manchester United. The United vintage of 1987 was very much a work in progress as the newly arrived Ferguson was just starting to decide who he wanted in his team. When City went to Old Trafford they were not favourites, but a win was by no means out of the question as United were struggling in the league.

Boosted by a week in Spain to relax and prepare for the match, City were ready to play out of their skins, and they did. An early Keith Houchen toe-poke, a scrambled effort, gave City a lead to defend, and they did so magnificently. United had plenty of possession, but with ex-City striker Terry Gibson misfiring, Coventry were able to hold on without too many alarms. This result got City noticed and by the time the fifth round draw paired them with high-flying Stoke City of the Second Division, some people were wondering how far the Sky Blues might go.

The same defence started City's third FA Cup tie in little over a month and that nicely settled unit, both organised and resolute, held firm against a tough Stoke outfit who pressed for much of the game. Late in the second period a Nick Pickering cross evaded David Phillips and it fell to Micky Gynn to deliver the solitary goal of a pulsating cup tie. The 8,000 away fans who made their way to the Victoria Ground that day left with a real sense of optimism about this City team; they had talented players, they had battlers, and now it seemed they had the bottle.

City were suddenly in the quarter-finals, away at Sheffield Wednesday. Roared on by 15,000 away fans, they produced some brilliant counter-attacking football to take the game to Wednesday. Regis opened the scoring with a powerful low finish, but before any second goal arrived, Gary Megson levelled matters. It was then that Lady Luck shone on Keith Houchen; his 20-yard shot was deflected in to give City a precious lead, and just 5 minutes later he pounced on a defensive error to slot home a decisive third. Houchen was on his knees in front of the delirious Sky Blue fans, who finally had an FA Cup semi-final to look forward to.

In the semi-final, Second Division Leeds threatened to wreck City's Wembley dreams as they led for nearly an hour, and but for Ogrizovic's courage and reflex saves, United might have been out of reach. Despite lots of possession, City could not score; star-man Regis typified the afternoon, miscuing shot after shot. With 20 minutes remaining, Dave Bennett, a winger not always renowned for chasing lost causes, chased like his life depended on it to reach a ball that was going harmlessly out. Bennett's cross was turned in by Micky Gynn and as the players celebrated you could almost see the fear drain from their faces. Houchen tiptoed in a second, and though Keith Edwards' goal took the game to an extra half-hour, City were gaining the upper hand. Bennett's scrambled third goal was the winner that set the Sky Blues on the way to Wembley for the very first time.

The final was a thriller for neutrals, but it had its share of heart-stopping moments for City fans. Trailing 1–0 after a minute and 2–1 at the interval, City had to do things the hard way. Once again Dave Bennett scored a major goal, this time to equalise Clive Allen's 1st-minute opener and City were competing well until shortly before half time when they conceded a sloppy second from a free-kick.

If the players were worried it did not show as they continued to press Spurs and when Keith Houchen made it 2–2 the goal was no surprise; the way in which he scored it though took everyone unawares. Houchen flew full-length to head home Bennett's cross, to register one of the most spectacular goals seen in any Wembley final. The source of City's winner was arguably an even bigger surprise. Early in extra time, of all people it was the midfield cruncher, Lloyd McGrath, who took off down the right wing. When he crossed, the ball deflected off Gary Mabbutt's knee, looped over Ray Clemence's arcing dive, before nestling neatly in the far corner of the Tottenham goal.

The good fortune was City's, but as most of the good football had been theirs too, few outside of North London begrudged City their first major trophy. The

104-year wait to become winners was over at last and the thousands who sang at Wembley, or danced all night in Broadgate, had seen Sky Blue history gloriously made.

CITY LEGENDS – JOHN SILLETT

Although John Sillett had a successful career as a full-back with Chelsea, Coventry and Plymouth, he is surely best known for his time as the Sky Blues' manager. The period Sillett was in charge brought City's only major trophy to date, as well as some relatively successful years of mid-table respectability.

Sillett's story began at Stamford Bridge in the 1950s where he played almost 100 games for Chelsea, before transferring to Jimmy Hill's resurgent Sky Blues in early 1962. For the next 4 years Sillett shared in some exciting times at Highfield Road as City were promoted to Division Two and reached an FA Cup quarter-final. In that time, Sillett developed his affection for the Sky Blues and struck up a rapport with another Sky Blues stalwart, the Iron Man himself, big George Curtis. Many years later, this partnership would serve City well once more.

Sillett coached at Bristol City for 6 years before serving his managerial apprenticeship at Hereford United. After guiding Hereford to the Third Division championship in 1976, Sillett settled back into coaching. He eventually returned to City, at Bobby Gould's invitation, in 1983. Things did not work out, however, and Sillett was soon looking for another job. Only the intervention of Don Mackay, 12 months later, brought Sillett's coaching skills to Highfield Road again. At the time, no one could have predicted the dizzy heights to which he would lead the club.

As City fought a desperate relegation battle in the spring of 1986, all seemed lost after a 5–0 thumping at Anfield with only three games left. Don Mackay resigned and the unlikely combination of John Sillett and George Curtis, ex-team-mates from the 1960s, took charge. The wily duo engineered a third successive last-gasp escape from relegation, but not many City fans were expecting a lot when it was announced that the pair would take permanent charge.

Sillett was chief coach in the partnership and he instantly revelled in the higher profile he had. As he was always good for a quote or two to the press, you could have been forgiven for thinking Sillett just talked a good game. It soon became apparent though, that he had his team playing a good game too.

Sillett and Curtis changed City's playing style, with more emphasis on a shorter passing game and immediate benefits were seen. City had started the season solidly; for the first time in years, they were hard to beat, and they were not out of the top ten before Christmas. Players who were previously underachieving – most notably Dave Bennett and Cyrille Regis – began to consistently play to their full ability.

Players of the time speak of the excellent team spirit Sillett fostered, and of how he took the trouble to treat them like adults. Certainly, his man-management skills were producing what City fans craved more than anything – good results. By the time City had reached their first FA Cup final in 1987, they had forged a steely determination with plenty of attacking flair, and it was a potent mix.

The final Wembley triumph over Spurs proved just how much Sillett had been able to get out of his players. Most of that FA Cup-winning team had already spent two or three disappointing years at Highfield Road, but they were able to reach their full potential in response to Sillett's boundless desire and enthusiasm.

Sillett's reward for the Wembley win was to be appointed team manger for the following three seasons. Although those 3 years were punctuated with a couple of horrendous cup defeats at Sutton and Northampton, the final league placings of tenth, seventh and twelfth were better than average for City's top-flight history. It was a time when City played attractive football for most of the time, particularly when David Speedie was on song, and they avoided any relegation scraps. In the context of City's top-flight history, they were heady days indeed.

For City fans, the abiding image of John Sillett will always be that of the jovial, rotund man jigging around Wembley with the cup. At times, he certainly might have played the part of the happy-go-lucky joker, but his bright and cheery nature should not mask the size of his achievement at Highfield Road. Sillett knew what he wanted from his players and he made sure he got it. The result was that City played with organisation, grit and flair to great effect. With a shrewdness that was often underestimated, Sillett gave Sky Blue fans everywhere a time to treasure.

THE BIGGEST BEATINGS!

City's record winning margin remains a 9–0 thrashing of Bristol City way back in 1934. 4-goal Clarrie Bourton led the way as City finished the season strongly in second place, with 100 league goals. It wasn't quite enough to clinch promotion that year though, free-scoring City were 7 points adrift of champions Norwich and had to wait 2 more years to secure promotion.

More recently though, larger winning margins have been rarer, but here are some of the biggest beatings handed out by the Sky Blues since promotion to Division One.

Coventry 8–0 Rushden & Diamonds, League Cup second round, 2 October 2002

A youthful Sky Blues team hit 4 in each half in Gary McAllister's first season as manager. Hopes were high that the returning McAllister could forge a challenge for promotion, but the season went rapidly downhill and City won just once in their last twenty-one matches.

Coventry 7–0 Macclesfield Town, FA Cup third round, 2 January, 1999

This was always a match that City were expected to win, as Town were in only their second full League campaign. However, the final margin was impressive. Darren Huckerby hit a second-half hat-trick as 7 goals ruined Macc's big day.

Coventry 7–2 Chester City, League Cup second round, 9 October 1985

In 90 minutes' action, Cyrille Regis scored 5 times, as many as he managed in his other thirty-seven matches that season! Regis had been some goalscorer at West Brom, but the night against Fourth Division Chester apart, his scoring touch seemed to have deserted him in a Sky Blue shirt. Within a year, though, Regis' fortunes were to be transformed under John Sillett's stewardship, and it was not just lower league teams who would fear him in the future.

Coventry 6–1 Sunderland, Division One, 27 April 1982

The youthful team Dave Sexton had assembled, spearheaded by Thompson and Hateley, finished the season strongly. City ran rings around Sunderland and the biggest win for nearly 30 years could have been even bigger; just a week later City were at it again, sharing the points with Southampton in a 5–5 thriller at The Dell.

Coventry 6–2 Derby, Championship, 30 April 2005

Highfield Road's farewell match could not have gone much better. Lingering thoughts of relegation were soon put to bed as City raced into a 4–0 half-time lead. Glorious sunshine bathed an emotional crowd as the curtain came down on 106 years of football at Highfield Road, and this was some encore.

Coventry 5–0 Blackburn, Premier League, 9 December 1995

Big-spending Blackburn were undone by an icy pitch, an orange ball and dazzling displays from Peter Ndlovu and Dion Dublin. Despite not having won for fourteen games, everything City tried worked and Rovers headed back to Ewood Park looking anything but defending champions.

Bolton Wanderers 1–5 Coventry, Premier League, 31 January 1998

The Huckerby and Dublin partnership was approaching the peak of its powers and the big man/quick man combination provided 4 of the 5 goals, following a deft opener from Noel Whelan. Confidence continued to soar in the Sky Blue ranks as they went on to set a new club record of seven successive wins.

Crewe Alexandra 1–6 Coventry, Division One, 9 January 2002

The comfortable win at Gresty Road left City in the play-off places and ready for an expected promotion push. Lee Hughes' hat-trick suggested he was hitting form at the right time and things looked bright. However, City soon faltered in unbelievable fashion, taking just one point out of the last twenty-one on offer and crashing out of the play-off picture. A decade later they have yet to make an impression on any promotion race.

Walsall 1–6 Coventry, Division One, 17 January 2004

The early signs under new manager Eric Black were looking good as City ripped into Walsall. Doubles from Morrell and McSheffrey suggested Black's team was going to have a greater emphasis on attacking intent; City fans were not complaining as they were treated to a 5-goal second half. Black's short stay in the hot-seat was characterised by some exciting attacking football, but mysteriously the Scot was soon to be replaced by the 'big name' Peter Reid, whose football was far from thrilling.

Coventry 6–1 Derby, Championship, 21 January 2006

Not even 12 months after Derby were roasted in the Highfield Road swansong, the Rams were battered again, this time conceding 5 times in the second period. The match was notable also for the first appearance of Dennis Wise, who became City's oldest debutant at the age of 39. Wise ran the show and his arrival signalled the start of a bright end-of-season spell for City, with Micky Adams leading the team to their highest final position, eighth, since returning to the second tier.

ROY OF THE ROVERS

By the time Keith Houchen joined City, in the summer of 1986, he was regarded as an archetypal, journeyman striker. Houchen had plied his trade for a handful of lower league clubs with some success, but, at the age of 26, he was in danger of never appearing on the game's biggest stages. Apart from converting a giant-killing penalty for York against Arsenal, the striker's name had never shone too brightly.

Houchen was determined to succeed in his first crack at top-flight football and his wholehearted efforts were soon apparent. He was strong in the air, had a good touch for a tall man and he could finish. However, an injury-blighted first 4 months meant the jury was still out on whether Houchen could prosper at the highest level.

Any lingering doubts about Houchen were soon dispelled, as the 1987 cup run took off. His scrambled winner at Old Trafford was soon followed by two solo strikes in a magical quarter-final against Sheffield Wednesday. Then, a semi-final strike against Leeds helped catapult City to their first ever FA Cup final. His diving header in the final, one of the best Wembley goals, cemented his place in FA Cup folklore.

In just 12 months, Houchen had gone from watching the FA Cup final in a working men's club, to assuming a starring role, playing the part of 'Roy of the Rovers' to perfection.

Almost inevitably, the giddy heights of 1987 were not sustained; the next season David Speedie took Houchen's place. Two more seasons at City reduced Houchen to a mere bit-part player, with only occasional appearances and goals. This was a harsh outcome for a man who was arguably one of City's best ever signings. City fans will always warmly remember Houchen – the man with The Midas Touch.

GIANTS KILLED

When the Sky Blues arrived at the picturesque Gander Green Lane to play non-league Sutton United in the third round of the 1989 FA Cup, the footballing world was a very different place. The Premier League did not exist, City had won the FA Cup just 18 months earlier and, incredible to think of it now, the Sky Blues were fourth in the top flight!

Days before the fixture, City had hammered Sheffield Wednesday 5–0, helped by a hat-trick of headers from a buoyant David Speedie, and so the confidence of both fans and players was sky high. On paper, it looked a straightforward tie, however Sutton had read a different script.

The part-timers scrapped ferociously and were edging what looked like being a goalless first half. Minutes before the break, City were undone by a near-post corner which was flicked on to the head of defender Matthew Rains. Although the fans did not enjoy their half-time cup of tea, the consensus in the ground was that it could only be a matter of time before City's quality come to the fore. Sure enough, 7 minutes after the restart David Phillips ran on to a Steve Sedgley pass before smartly converting. However, things were not on an even keel for long; just 6 minutes later City were again found wanting at defending a set-piece. A cleverly pulled back corner and cross gave wide man Matthew Hanlon a volley he, and City fans, will never forget.

In the final half-hour City woke up and chased the game. Regis was an inch away from equalising, substitute

Houchen hit the bar and Sedgley managed to hit both bar and post on the rebound. That said though, Sutton still created some opportunities of their own and when the curtain came down on City calamitous afternoon, few who were present could dispute Sutton were worthy winners.

IN BETWEEN THE STICKS!

No-one can better Steve Ogrizovic as City's leading number one over the years; the fact that all of his mammoth 601 first-team appearances came as a part of top-flight City teams is a record no other keeper has come close to. However, Oggy is far from being the only interesting character who has occupied the space in between the City sticks.

Considering he never played a first-team match for the Sky Blues, it is surprising how many times ex-broadcaster, ex-Green Party spokesman and reputed 'Son of God' David Icke has been referred to as an ex-Coventry City goalkeeper. Icke was a promising youth goalie for the Sky Blues between 1969 and 1971, appearing on the losing City side in the 1970 FA Youth Cup final against a Tottenham team which included Graeme Souness and Steve Perryman. He was also once on the substitutes' bench for the first team, in the infamous 6–1 drubbing against Munich, however, the onset of arthritis restricted Icke's time at the club and within a couple of years he had retired from professional football.

Icke took up a successful career as a sports journalist, becoming a well-known TV commentator in the 1980s. However, as time went on, he became better known for his books and broadcasts on what he calls the 'nature of consciousness'. For those City fans who have often wondered what exactly goalkeepers are thinking about when the ball is up the other end of the pitch, perhaps Icke provides some answers!

Raddy Avramovic enjoyed only a brief City career, playing eighteen first-team matches in the 1983/84 season. After a steady start, his spell became notable for a sequence of unfortunate errors; conceding a goal-kick against Watford and then turning in a below-par performance against Stoke City, during which Avramovic was badly at fault for a couple of goals, all infuriated Gould. The manager publicly declared he would never select Avramovic again and stuck to his word. The now ex-keeper headed back to Yugosalvia to study law. Years later he re-emerged as the successful coach of Singapore, hopefully being a little kinder to any errant goalkeepers than some were to him!

More recently, Keiren Westwood rightly earned himself a reputation for being the best keeper outside of the Premiership. From his first matches for the club, Westwood stood out as more capable than any keeper City have employed since Ogrizovic's retirement. Few mistakes, fantastic athleticism and phenomenal reflexes very quickly made Ireland's number two Coventry's number one. A big future is expected for the man from Manchester.

CITY LEGENDS – DION DUBLIN

The bare facts about Dion Dublin's 4 years at the Sky Blues speak for themselves: he was top scorer each season, he won the Golden Boot in 1998 and he won four England caps too; all this was achieved on the way to becoming the Sky Blues' leading top-flight scorer, with 71 strikes. It looks impressive on paper and it was a very impressive time in his career.

Dublin was snapped up from Manchester United reserves in the autumn of 1994 by an astute Phil Neal. He began his City career like an express train, netting in his first few games. This quickly established Dublin as a firm terrace favourite, and his name was chanted with gusto almost immediately.

At the beginning of his City career, Dublin had a reputation, going back to his days in a very direct Cambridge team, of being just a big target man and not much more. That impression of Dublin was wrong. Although his game matured considerably while with the Sky Blues, Dublin was never just a one-dimensional player. He had terrific heading ability, he could hold the ball up and cleverly link play, as well as finish most chances that fell his way. He arrived as a more than useful striker, and by the time he left, he was a sought-after England player who had polished his skills to such an extent that his transfer value had nearly trebled.

Typically, Dublin's years at City coincided with relegation scraps and only in his last full year, 1997/98, did those fears disappear. Before that it was often backs-to-the-wall brinkmanship, but somehow Dublin seemed to thrive on it all; leading the team by both example and exhortation, he dragged the most he could from his team-mates. With a regular goalscorer in the team, City always had a fighting chance of surviving their relegation scraps, and they just about did.

As well as being a consistent scorer, Dublin enjoyed many highlights in his stay at the club: his crucial winning goal at Anfield in 1997; his goal weeks later at White Hart Lane that helped secure an unbelievable escape; and an opening-day hat-trick against Ruud Gullit's stylish Chelsea all spring to mind. In fact that treble set the tone for a terrific final campaign as Dublin worked in tandem with the dangerous and speedy Darren Huckerby.

Between them they scored 38 goals and for a time, their pairing was a dream ticket. While Huckerby's twisting runs turned defenders inside out, Dublin's muscle and touch often turned them upside down! In a 3–1 FA Cup win at Liverpool both men produced one of their finest matches in Sky Blue. Dublin was the focal point for every City attack, holding the ball up like he had it on a string, while Huckerby tiptoed around the Liverpool defence like an expert burglar.

Sadly, the pairing was destined not to last, as Dublin inevitably attracted envious glances from other clubs. His eventual transfer to rivals Aston Villa certainly grated with many fans, but it should not overshadow the huge contribution he made to the City cause. He played deep into his 30s and for many clubs, but it was in the Sky Blue shirt that he produced his best.

SHORT & SWEET

Over the years, particularly in the era of the loanee, many players have enjoyed only the briefest of stays with the Sky Blues. One or two fleeting visitors have, however, managed to leave a lasting impression . . .

On the morning of 1 September 1979, rookie goalie Steve Murcott had kept a clean sheet for the City youth team and was getting ready to enjoy an afternoon off watching the first team take on Norwich. When established number one Jim Blyth hurt his back in the warm-up, Murcott was the only other Sky Blues keeper at Highfield Road and was duly called up to make the most dramatic of debuts. Although Murcott kept his second clean sheet of the day, it was not enough to secure even one more outing for the first team. Murcott was left with just his memories and the indisputable fact that he never once let a goal in during the whole of his City career!

When Blackburn Rovers visited a snow-covered Highfield Road in December 1995, they found a City team filled with attacking potential, but lacking in points and leaking goals. To help plug the gaps in defence, Ron Atkinson had just drafted in the experienced Chris Whyte for a month's loan; it was to be his only outing in Sky Blue. The match saw Atkinson's expensively assembled team finally hit form; Premier League champions Blackburn gave away more gifts than Santa as they were buried under a 5–0 avalanche. However, as defenders regained fitness, and the team picked up points, Whyte's City career stalled on that solitary, snowy, dreamlike appearance – things could never have been so good again!

Briefer still was the playing time enjoyed by City striker Mick Harford. Having been brought in by Bobby Gould in the summer of 1993 and handed the number nine shirt, hopes were high that the veteran striker could use his considerable strength to good effect with goal-grabber Mick Quinn. Sadly, injuries reduced Harford's time on the pitch to just 15 minutes in 13 months. In that time, however, he rose magnificently to head a winning goal against Newcastle United, leaving Harford with a strike rate unlikely to ever be bettered – 1 goal every 15 minutes!

THE SKY'S THE LIMIT

A long, long time ago, in a galaxy far, far away, there was a world without Sky TV. Back then, football junkies had only the titbits offered on terrestrial television with which to feed their footballing appetites; there were no

Monday night matches, there was no *Soccer Saturday* and there was no *Super Sunday* (future historians could be forgiven for mixing up Rupert Murdoch with God, when it comes to deciding who invented the days of the week). However, everything about televised football was about to change.

In 1992, BSKYB paid over £300million for the right to screen live matches from the newly formed Premier League, meaning for the first time you would have to pay to watch English league football on your TV. With an expensive new product to sell, the marketing team at Sky were about to go into overdrive.

Once again under the aegis of Bobby Gould, City had started the season in blistering fashion winning five out of their first seven matches. Eager not to miss the early-season headliners, Sky debuted at Highfield Road for a fixture against Spurs. While much excitement was on the pitch, far more gimmickry was in the air.

The *Coventry Evening Telegraph* had advertised the match as a Sky spectacular, and they were right. A decent game was prefaced with dancers and parachutists and to many it seemed there was something in this satellite TV lark. A new family orientated way of watching football, complete with fun and frolics, was being served up. But there was more to come.

The pre-match publicity had promised a big-name guest appearance at the interval – a sort of insurance policy against a dreary match. When the big name turned out to be the little singing scouser Sonia (a future Eurovision contestant), the gimmickry soon turned to mimicry and the full fury of the Highfield Road crowd was vented upon her. Sky have of course, gone on to set the highest standards in sports presentation, but even they had to start somewhere. Nearly two decades on, Sonia is still waiting for her second invite to wow the Sky Blue Army.

CITY LEGENDS – BRIAN BORROWS

For just over 12 years, Brian 'Bugsy' Borrows helped to plug some of the gaps in City's defence. From the summer of 1985 to the autumn of 1997, Borrows was an integral part of a City defence that often creaked and groaned, and, only occasionally, sank without trace.

Borrows arrived at City from Bolton for the modest sum of £80,000 and, considering he went on to spend 12 years at Highfield Road, that represents quite a bargain. In that time, Borrows played mostly as a right-back, with the odd spell in the middle. Wherever he played though, there were common features to Borrows' game.

Borrows was not an aggressive defender; his game was never about scything down an opponent and launching them into the crowd; Borrows simply did not need to play that way. Although he was never blessed with great pace, he had an uncanny knack of being in the right place at the right time. Positional sense is vital for a full-back, and Bugsy's resembled that of a chess grandmaster. It seemed that he could anticipate his opponents' next moves before they had even made them. His tackling wasn't bad either. His deft nudges and pushes of the ball were often just enough to nick the ball away from any speedy raider. He timed his challenges perfectly.

Despite a first year of dodging relegation, things improved rapidly and Borrows became a cornerstone of the FA Cup-winning team. However, after missing only one match all season, Borrows was cruelly injured a week before the 1987 FA Cup final, and had to miss the biggest match in City's history.

Although he never got the international recognition his ability merited, Bugsy can still look back with a lot of pride on a dozen unbroken years in the top flight. For a City defender, he had a rare combination of qualities, a good touch, quick feet and slide rule tackling. Borrows really was a man to depend upon in a crisis, and City, very often did.

THE ENTERTAINERS – DARREN HUCKERBY

In the autumn of 1996, struggling City were short of fire-power to supplement an out-of-sorts Dion Dublin. To remedy the developing crisis, Strachan smartly snapped up Darren Huckerby, from Newcastle's reserves, for around £1 million; he was renowned for being quick and having half an eye for goal, two qualities the goal-shy Sky Blues were crying out for.

In his third full appearance Huckerby grabbed his first goal for City, racing onto a pinpoint Kevin Richardson pass to set City on the way to victory against a talented Newcastle team. It was a goal that straight away told us much about Huckerby; on his day he could finish, he had fantastic pace and, if he got the right service, he could be deadly. Although that season was a desperate battle against relegation, the portents for the Dublin and Huckerby partnership were good; probably not since the days of Ian Wallace and Mick Ferguson, some 20 years before, had City possessed two front men whose styles suited each other so well.

The following year was a breakthrough one for Huckerby, who played a starring role in high-profile wins against Tottenham, Manchester United and Liverpool. Firstly, City thrashed a poor Tottenham team 4–0, and Huckerby was tremendous; he fizzed and sparkled all over the pitch and scored twice. His first goal was hit so hard it looked like it might knock the whole goal frame over; Huckerby had hit the ball the way Roy Race used to belt them in every week for Melchester Rovers.

If that was good, the very next home game against Manchester United was real comic-strip stuff as Huckerby scored a spectacular last-minute winner to sink league leaders United. With his confidence sky high, Huckerby then went up to Liverpool for a cup tie and proceeded to dribble his way past half the Liverpool defence before scoring, from what even a maths teacher would have to call an impossible angle. After a magical month, City's star was rising and Huckerby was dazzling.

Unfortunately, when Dublin left early the next season, Huckerby had a less productive supply line and the team struggled to match the previous year's success. It's debatable whether Huckerby ever quite regained the heights of 1998 in a City shirt, or indeed anybody else's, after he then left in the summer of 1999. Throughout his City career though, Huckerby had the tricks, the speed and the eye for goal, which every defender hates, but every fan loves. With his willingness to take on any defender in sight, Huckerby was a popular figure at Highfield Road because more than anything, he simply entertained.

CITY'S BEST LEAGUE CUP RUNS – PART III

1989/90

Round 2, L1	(A)	Grimsby Town	1–3
Round 2, L2	(H)	Grimsby Town	3–0
Round 3	(A)	QPR	2–1
Round 4	(A)	Manchester City	1–0
QF	(A)	Sunderland	0–0
QF (r)	(H)	Sunderland	5–0
SF, L1	(A)	Nottingham Forest	1–2
SF, L2	(H)	Nottingham Forest	0–0

After an inauspicious start to the League Cup campaign at Grimsby, City soon improved. Away wins at top-flight QPR and Man City put the Sky Blues in the quarter-finals against in-form Division Two Sunderland. A replay was needed to progress, but the 5–0 home win was a spectacular night for emerging striker Steve Livingston who bagged 4 goals. A controversial first-leg defeat to Nottingham Forest left the decider at Highfield Road evenly poised. City pressed hard and Regis hit the bar, but it was not to be City's year, as Forest went on to claim the trophy for a second successive year.

1990/91

Round 2, L1	(H)	Bolton Wanderers	4–2
Round 2, L2	(A)	Bolton Wanderers	3–2
Round 3	(H)	Hull City	3–0
Round 4	(H)	Nottingham Forest	5–4
QF	(H)	Sheffield Wednesday	0–1

A desperately disappointing defeat to Second Division Wednesday was hard to take for supporters who had just begun to set their sights on a return to Wembley's twin towers. City fans had witnessed one of the all-time great matches at Highfield Road in the previous round, when City had played magnificently to put out the holders Nottingham Forest in a 9-goal thriller. Wednesday went on to Wembley where they shocked Manchester United 1–0 to take the trophy out of the top division.

BEATING THE BIG BOYS

Coventry City 4–0 Liverpool, 10 December 1983
This was one of Coventry's finest footballing hours. It was a day when the defending league champions were simply blown apart at Highfield Road. This was the season when Liverpool went on to do the treble of League Championship, League Cup and European Cup. The Liverpool team included some of their greatest ever players: Dalglish, Souness and Hansen were used to steamrollering opponents. City, in contrast, were fielding Bobby Gould's bargain basement team assembled from the lower leagues. The Sky Blues' leading lights of the time were Sam Allardyce, Raddy Avramovic and Nicky Platnauer; hardly names to worry the all-conquering Merseysiders. On paper, it should have been no contest, but as all good punters know, no game has ever been won on paper.

The season had been going well for City, with several away wins, and a place in the top ten being maintained. However, Liverpool were so far ahead as to be out of sight in those days, and it was difficult to see beyond honourable defeat. Within a minute of kick-off though, City had scored. The goal was bizarre in the extreme; a header from a floored player, the tireless Platnauer, who bundled a Grobbelaar spill over the line. It was that sort of day.

City scored a second after 20 minutes. Terry Gibson fired home after Dave Bennett's run had caused havoc in a bewildered Liverpool defence. Gibson was a diminutive forward, who that day gave a masterclass in pinching space in the penalty area. Just before half time Gibson had his second after another fumble from the now prostrate Grobbelaar. The Highfield Road regulars tucked into their Bovrils with the footballing Gods quite literally on their knees!

Sometimes in matches where one side is goals ahead at the interval, the second period can be an anti-climax. There were no such problems that day though as City maintained their good work. With defence and midfield outstanding, some crisp tackling and speedy attacks ensured the Liverpool recovery never got out of first gear.

Some fine goalkeeping kept the score at 3–0 until 10 minutes from time. Then, the shortest man on the pitch, tiny Terry Gibson, won a header against England's Phil Neal on the halfway line. From there he raced on to face Grobbelaar and beat him with a confident shot off the far post. The West End went wild, Gibson's name was up in lights and excitable *Match of the Day* commentator John Motson sounded like he had been launched into orbit.

At the final whistle the unprecedented chorus of, 'We're gonna win the league!' broke out in parts of the stadium. Liverpool boss Joe Fagan claimed that City were, 'genuine title contenders', and it seemed anything was possible after this stirring victory.

Perhaps predictably, Coventry City struggled to win another match until the following April and the dizzy heights of fourth became a definite mirage in another barren year. Somehow though, the later disappointments of the year didn't matter so much; on one freezing, dreary December afternoon, Highfield Road never felt warmer.

CITY'S BEST FA CUP RUNS – PART V

1997/98

Round 3	(A)	Liverpool	3–1
Round 4	(H)	Derby County	2–0
Round 5	(A)	Aston Villa	1–0
QF	(H)	Sheffield United	1–1
QF (r)	(A)	Sheffield United	1–1 (aet)

Lost 3–1 on penalties

Having just beaten Manchester United 3–2 in a Christmas spectacular, the Sky Blues were full of confidence as they set off to Anfield for a third round tie. Despite conceding early, City played with a purpose and were a threat throughout. Another spectacular Huckerby goal was followed by others from Dublin and Telfer, as City turned Liverpool over in one of their best perfomances under Gordon Strachan. A straighforward home win against Derby in round four set up the exciting prospect of a trip to Villa Park in the last 16.

Record signing Viorel Moldovan had recently joined for £3.25 million, but until the trip to Villa, he had struggled to make much of an impression. That all changed the minute he knocked in a loose rebound from a George Boateng shot in the 72nd minute. Moldovan put his name into the Sky Blue history books by being the scorer of the winner the first time City ever won at Villa Park. The victory was just reward for a tigerish display, laced with attacking intent – inspired by Boateng, City were just too good for Villa that day. After waiting 50 years to win on their rivals' home patch, this was a special afternoon for the travelling City fans.

The reward for the Villa Park heroics was a seemingly kind home draw against Division One outfit Sheffield

United. City had won a record-breaking seven matches on the trot and with Huckerby and Dublin scaring the life out of Premiership defences, the portents were good.

A goal apiece in the first half was not added to in the second period though, and when United nearly stole victory after a late Ogrizovic blunder, a replay suited City. Again, in the match at Bramall Lane, City started well; Paul Telfer scored within 10 minutes and City gained in confidence as the match wore on. Fifth-round hero Moldovan missed a great chance to double the lead, but for most of the match City still looked good for the semi-final against Newcastle. Moments from full-time, however, disaster struck and David Holdsworth equalised for United, taking the tie into extra time.

The longer the extra period went on without any further goals, the more likely the lottery of penalty kicks became. When the final whistle blew to indicate the shoot-out, fingers were crossed that the veteran Ogrizovic could perform one more miracle. To his credit, the keeper saved the first United kick, but sadly, City missed three and the best cup run in a decade was over. The romance of the cup stayed in Sheffield, and departing City fans left for home, just a little broken-hearted.

2008/09

Round 3	(H)	Kidderminster Harriers	2–0
Round 4	(A)	Torquay United	1–0
Round 5	(A)	Blackburn Rovers	2–2
Round 5 (r)	(H)	Blackburn Rovers	1–0
QF	(H)	Chelsea	0–2

Chris Coleman's team safely negotiated two rounds of lower league opposition before pitching up at Blackburn's Ewood Park. Just a year earlier City had enjoyed a spectacular 4–1 cup upset at Blackburn and hopes were high that they could do it again.

The tie at Ewood was eventful even before it began; half the City players had been laid low with a virus and keeper Keiren Westwood pulled out during the pre-match warm up. However, illness and an early Blackburn goal did not put off the Sky Blues, and they turned the match around to lead 2–1 going into injury time. When Rovers equalised in the last moments, it looked as if City's best chance might have gone, though at least there was a money-spinning replay to look forward to.

Promising striker Leon Best scored the replay's only goal in arguably the best night match seen at the Ricoh Arena. Wearing a protective face mask, Best had been dubbed both 'Zorro' and the 'Phantom of the Opera', on account of his appearance, but there was nothing theatrical about his firmly planted header, which took City through to the quarter-final of the FA Cup once again.

The plum tie against Chelsea guaranteed a capacity crowd and the growing excitement in the city of Coventry was hard to ignore. However, if the supporters were getting carried away with hopes of another impressive upset, Chelsea were not. The Londoners put in an impressively professional performance, restricting City thoughout the game and expertly taking their own chances, the 2–0 scoreline hardly reflected the distance between the teams.

CITY STALWARTS

The ten leading appearance makers for Coventry City are:

1	Steve Ogrizovic	1984–2000	601
2	George Curtis	1955–69	538
3	Mick Coop	1966–81	492
4	Brian Borrows	1985–97	477
5	Bill Glazier	1964–75	395
6	Mick Kearns	1957–68	382
7	Richard Shaw	1995–2006	362
8	Tommy Hutchison	1972–81	355
9	George Mason	1931–52	350
10	Roy Kirk	1951–60	345

The top ten City appearance makers are spread quite evenly through the decades, ranging from the 1930s onwards. While all the names to make the list have enjoyed lengthy associations with the club, it might be surprising to see that even the likes of Coop, Curtis and Ogrizovic have not spent the longest time on City's books. That distinction goes to George Mason, who represented City over an astonishing 21-year period. Had the war not intervened, Mason would have been much higher up the list of all-time appearance makers. In the modern game however, with fleeting stays at clubs often the norm, Mason's record for longevity is unlikely to ever be bettered.

TAKING A PUNT

Goalkeepers scoring goals from open play is supposed to be a bit like Halley's Comet – if you live long enough, you might just get a glimpse of this strange phenomenon. Funnily enough though, in less than three years, City fans were treated to two once-in-a-lifetime strikes.

On a freezing January day in 1984, City hosted a Watford side who were enjoying life in the top flight. The Hornets were causing a stir with the goals of Maurice Johnston and big George Reilly and their season was to take them all the way to an FA Cup final appearance.

However, thoughts of Wembley were probably far from goalie Steve Sherwood's mind when he picked the ball up in front of the West End ready to launch an early first-half attack. Under future England manager Graham Taylor, Sherwood's long punt to the head of George Reilly for Maurice Johnston to feed off was proving an effective weapon. On this occasion though, Sherwood hit the jackpot. A freakish wind took hold of his mighty kick and before City's then number one, Raddy Avramovic, could decide on the expected trajectory of the ball, it had bounced over him and into the East Terrace net. A stunned home crowd were silenced, while a disbelieving Sherwood smiled wider than the Watford Gap.

Fast-forward to the winter of 1986 and City by now had the impressive Steve Ogrizovic guarding their net. Oggy had almost immediately started to carve out a reputation for his safe hands and reliability, but not for goalscoring!

Prior to a league fixture at Sheffield Wednesday in October 1986, City's number one had got talking with his deputy, Jake Findlay, about their next opponents, and in particular, the opposing keeper Martin Hodge. The fact that Hodge tended to sometimes stray a long way out of his goal was picked up on, as it meant could be vulnerable to a giant clearance.

As the game was played in atrocious weather, with plenty of rain and wind, Oggy had the opportunity to test out the training ground theory. Halfway through the second period, with the teams drawing 1–1, Ogrizovic collected the ball in his own penalty area and launched an almighty punt towards Hodge's goal. Both fans and players looked on in astonishment as the ball travelled an enormous distance before bouncing towards the Wednesday keeper and arcing over him into the net off a post. Typically, Oggy was modest about his achievement, but with that kick he joined a very select club of keepers who have scored from open play with a goal-kick. Ogrizovic became the first, and so far, only City keeper to trouble the scorers.

THE ONE AND ONLY …
JIMMY HILL

In the whole history of Coventry City, few figures have influenced the football club as much as Jimmy Hill. He arrived, in November 1961, at an ailing Third Division team, on its knees after FA Cup defeat to non-league King's Lynn, and, though he had no management experience, he had some things even more valuable – a vision of where he wanted to take Coventry City and the drive to get them there.

In his first full season Hill immediately made his mark; he rebranded Coventry City as the Sky Blues, cleverly drawing a line under previous years of mediocrity, while promising something new and fresh. City's new all sky blue kit was English football's first one-colour strip and it immediately made the team stand out for how they looked, but it was not long before they stood out for how they played as well.

Hill had money to spend from chairman Derrick Robins and shrewdly reshaped the team with key signings including John Sillett and goalscorer Terry Bly. Quite aside from his good PR, his reworking of the 'Eton Boating Song' and his 'pop and crisps' parties, it was on the playing field where Hill really began to earn his money as the team were successful again. In his first full season, the Sky Blues finished fourth and enjoyed a memorable run to the FA Cup quarter-finals. When Hill delivered the Third Division championship the following season City fans began to look upwards once again; the dream of top-flight football that had looked possible, even likely, before the war was back on the agenda.

It took Hill two seasons to make City challengers in Division Two, but after narrowly missing out on promotion in 1966, a majestic campaign in 1967, including an unbeaten league run of over 5 months, propelled the Sky Blues to the top flight at last. Sadly for City fans on the eve of their Division One debut, Hill announced he would be leaving to work in television, and though he went on to develop a long and distinguished broadcasting career, City fans of a certain age can not help but wonder what he might have achieved had he stayed on.

Hill did go back to Coventry, first as Managing Director, and later as Chairman, but he was never quite able to recreate the excitement the club had enjoyed during his time as manager. Instead, it was to be the steady success of maintaining a cherished top-flight spot which would mostly occupy City managers for more than three decades.

However, the fact that generations of Coventry City fans would grow up following the Sky Blues as a First Division outfit at all, was, more than anything, Hill's tremendous legacy. He took over at a shocking low-point, he transformed the whole club and he turned the team into winners – people have had statues raised in their honour for less!

THE TRAPDOOR OPENS

A proud run of thirty-four consecutive years of top-flight football ended for Coventry City in May 2001. At the time, the run was the fourth-longest of any club in the top division; only Arsenal, Everton and Liverpool had maintained a place at football's top table for a longer period.

Following a tortuous year blighted by few goals and even fewer wins, fate took the Sky Blues to Villa Park in the penultimate game of the 2000/01 season. A late resurgence in the team's fortunes had offered hope of another improbable escape, but desperate for points and with an eye on other team's results, City went to Villa Park dancing once again on the relegation trapdoor.

This time though there was to be no escape and, on a sunny afternoon at Villa Park, an early 2–0 lead dissolved into a 3–2 defeat; City's exit from the Premier League was confirmed. Quite simply, that year's Sky Blue vintage was poor and too many rival teams were just that little bit better.

In all that time at the pinnacle of English football, Coventry became renowned as almost perennial relegation battlers; the startling statistic of ten last-day escapes from varying relegation threats, certainly added weight to the notion. Sadly though, the reality was that even creaking gates do sometimes keel over.

From the days of Jimmy Hill's promotion heroes to the strugglers of the 1970s, from the escapologists of the mid-1980s to the never-say-dies of the 1990s, the team's recent relegation battles had all been won. Somehow, the fact that successive teams and managers had managed to contrive so many unlikely escapes for so long made the final exit even more disappointing; relegation was a bitter pill to swallow.

SUGAR DADDY

While the fans of Chelsea, Manchester City and many other Premiership clubs have got used to tucking in and gorging themselves on the millions being splashed about their owners, followers of less galactic clubs, like the Sky Blues, could be forgiven just a hint of envy.

City fans, like most up and down the country, would of course welcome the massive injection that cash benefactors bring with them. Whether it be the local boy turned-good who wants to put something back into his hometown, like Blackburn's Jack Walker, or the distant and recent convert, like Roman Abramovich, who just needs a new toy to play with, which fans would not warmly welcome a chairman loaded with bucketfuls of cash?

In the autumn of 2004, it seemed, for a short time, that City fans' hopes and dreams of a dashing benefactor might just have been about to come true. Enter Mr Joe Dhinsa. This local boy had not just made good, but, according to his own publicity, had made so much cash that he would scarcely miss the many millions he was planning to sink into the struggling Sky Blues.

After the galloping publicity surrounding Dhinsa's hoped-for takeover, the subsequent failure of the bid to materialise left many fans forlorn. Opinions of Dhinsa varied from Billy Liar fantasist to smart businessman who knew a bad deal when he saw one. Whichever verdict City fans subscribe to, for a short time at least, Dhinsa managed to set many Sky Blue pulses racing, with dreams of future glories.

Though City's potential sugar daddy turned out to be less sugar and more Canderel, bearing in mind the recent experiences of Leeds United and others who 'lived the dream', a little reality might yet help the Sky Blues go a long way.

THE GOOD, THE BAD AND THE UGLY

Over the years, Coventry City managers have come in all shapes and sizes. Here are some of the most famous and infamous who have sat in the Sky Blue hot-seat.

Noel Cantwell (1967–72)

Noel Cantwell arrived at Highfield Road with an almost impossible task – filling the gaping hole left by the talismanic Jimmy Hill. City fans had been treated to glorious highs under Hill's stewardship and whoever took over would have suffered in comparison. Cantwell himself famously talked about the 'ghost of Jimmy Hill' following him around, but even any spooks lingering at Highfield Road would have had to give Cantwell credit for what he went on to achieve.

In 4½ years at the helm, most importantly Cantwell kept the Sky Blues in the top flight. There were narrow scrapes along the way in his first two seasons, but the Irishman put out teams that scrapped and fought, and just about scrambled to safety. Cantwell had enjoyed trophy-winning days as a player at Manchester United and while those heights were not scaled at City, he did deliver the club's best ever league placing, sixth in 1970, and a European campaign the following season; Cantwell's City made solid progress.

Gordon Milne (1972–81)

Gordon Milne arrived at City after a distinguished playing career; an England international and twice a league champion with Liverpool under Bill Shankly, he had impressive credentials. For his first two seasons Milne managed side-by-side with Joe Mercer, who had himself enjoyed great success managing Manchester City to both the league championship, plus domestic and European cups. Although the pairing were unable to steer City out of the bottom half of the table, the team reached both FA and League Cup quarter-finals in successive seasons and were providing the fans with more cheer than gloom.

When Mercer left to take charge of the national team in 1974, Milne stepped up to take sole charge of the team and he went on to hold that position for seven whole seasons, making him City's longest-serving top-flight manager. Although City only once broke into the top half of the league throughout Milne's tenure (the Wallace and Ferguson inspired vintage of 1977/78), he was instrumental in establishing the club as part of the First Division landscape. In Milne's time there was only one perilously close relegation battle (the controversial 1977 campaign), and there were plenty of good young players coming through the ranks. Most notably, there was almost a first Wembley cup final – City narrowly lost out to West Ham in the 1981 League Cup semis. Milne's teams were not often spectacular, but like their manager they were solid and steady.

Dave Sexton (1981–3)

Dave Sexton arrived in time for what was meant to be a new era for the Sky Blues. Highfield Road had just been redeveloped into English football's first all-seater stadium, and in Thompson, Hateley, Thomas and Gillespie, Sexton had inherited plenty of promising young players in whom hopes were high.

An opening-day win over Manchester United set the tone for an erratic first season; Sexton's team could turn on the style, but maintaining it over a period of games was another matter. Despite reaching another cup quarter-final, a post-Christmas slump edged City towards the drop zone, but the team rallied and finished strongly, dispatching Sunderland 6–1 and drawing 5–5 with Southampton within a week.

The experience gained from Sexton's first year seemed to be being put to great effect the following year as City climbed to fifth spot by Christmas. A tremendous home record signalled that Sexton's boys seemed to be coming of age and the future looked bright.

Once again though, the Sky Blue train came off the rails and a run of thirteen games without a win, from February to May (coinciding with the sale of star striker Garry Thompson) gave everyone some serious relegation worries. A vital win at Stoke averted relegation, but the club was in a mess, allowing their young stars to leave en masse in the summer, after first sacking Sexton. Quite what else he could have done with a young, but inexperienced team, low gates and no money remains a mystery!

Bobby Gould (1983–4)

When the ex-City striker Bobby Gould returned to Highfield Road as team manager in the summer of 1983, it was a widely welcomed appointment. Gould had been was an original homegrown hero; he was the busy, bustling striker in City's promotion-winning side from the 1960s and was still popular with the Sky Blue faithful.

On arrival, Gould might have felt like taking a crash course in crisis management as eight of the previous season's first-team squad were allowed to leave to various highest bidders in the summer. With no team and little spare cash, the prospects for extending City's stay in the top flight looked grim. Luckily though, Gould had both a passion for his hometown team and an emerging eye for spotting talent in the lower leagues.

Gould brought in good players who would go on to become future cup-winners – Bennett, Gynn and Peake – all arrived that summer. The change in personnel was not the only difference though; City had started to win. In early December, Gould's team stunned the footballing world with a 4–0 thumping of champions Liverpool. This was the same Liverpool who had won the championship for the previous two years and who would go on to win the Milk Cup, League Championship and European Cup within the next 6 months.

Unfortunately, those heady days did not last. The turn of the year saw City go into freefall; they tumbled down the league like a Christmas number one crashes out of the January charts. In April, City found themselves on a run of thirteen games without a win. Narrow defeats had started to be replaced by some 4-goal pastings and things looked grim. People believed Gould's previously inspired team had found their true level at last, and, after an appalling 8–2 reversal at Southampton, it seemed difficult to argue.

City stuttered to their final game more in hope than in expectation of another escape. Goals from on-loan Mick Ferguson, and winger Dave Bennett, secured City the win they needed for another year in Division One. The new season saw old struggles return and Gould was sacked in the December of the following season after a dismal run, which saw City unable to dredge themselves out of the bottom three. With goals being leaked by the bucket-load, and no signs of discernible progress having been made since the previous season, a parting of the ways had been becoming more and more likely.

Don Mackay (1984–6)

After a desperate run of results, Booby Gould was sacked just after Christmas of 1984, leaving his assistant Don Mackay to take over team affairs. While the caricature of the dour, unsmiling Scot could have been invented with Mackay in mind, he soon managed to cobble together some victories to raise hopes of avoiding the drop. Postponed matches left City playing catch-up to complete their fixtures and the team had three games still to play after their nearest rivals Norwich had finished 8 points ahead.

Incredibly, and against all expectations, City won three successive matches to stay up, it was a Lazarus of a comeback and was Mackay's finest time at Highfield Road. The following season saw some ups, but more downs and City struggled to break out of the bottom third of the table all year. With three games left Mackay resigned, seemingly in acknowledgement of the desperate trouble that City were in; Curtis and Sillett stepped in to save the day as Don Mackay became another short-lived manager in increasingly turbulent times for the club.

Terry Butcher (1990–2)

Terry Butcher took over the Highfield Road hot seat just 3 years after City's FA Cup triumph. The chief architect of the cup win, coach John Sillett, had been unceremoniously sacked after results had dipped and in response, the City board took the radical step of appointing a high-profile, but untried and unproven player/manager. Only six months earlier Butcher had been the defensive kingpin on which England had leaned in their exciting march to the semi-finals of the Italia '90 World Cup.

When Butcher landed at Highfield Road he found a team in need of some fairly major surgery. Many of the FA Cup winners had already left, and one or two more were coming to the natural end of their City careers. A fresh approach was needed in the long term, but, in the short term, results were needed as City had slipped to a lowly fifteenth. Had their abysmal away form of just one victory all season been replicated at Highfield Road, City would have sunk without trace. However, Butcher's boys managed to conjure up some impressive home performances in an unbeaten home run of fourteen matches. The Boxing Day taming of a Spurs side, bolstered by Italia '90 stars Gascoigne and Lineker was arguably the pick of some strong home performances.

Butcher's second season was bleak in the extreme. Scoring goals became a major problem and wins were rare. Perhaps the most disappointing aspect was the manner in which the team played; the eye-catching, passing style fostered by John Sillett seemed to have been largely disregarded. City were increasingly predictable; they made a lot of effort; they played a lot of long balls, but they consistently lacked the necessary craft and guile to break down even moderate defences.

By the time Cambridge United visited in the third round of the FA Cup, people's patience with Butcher was running out. The match was about as ugly a game of football as you could ever find. Both teams attempted to be even more direct than their opponents, with the result that it looked as if the players had secretly switched codes to rugby. Although City drew that wretched tie, it was not enough for Butcher, who was sacked before the replay. With hindsight, the appointment was a high-risk strategy that was probably always doomed; appointing a manager with no previous management experience at all was inviting trouble.

Don Howe (1992)

After Terry Butcher's reign ended in his sacking, City appointed the hugely experienced Don Howe to steer them to safety. In the 4 months he had the job he certainly organised the team and for a time made them harder to beat, though four consecutive 0–0 draws was hardly a high point. Although the class of 1992 was not a vintage year, just three wins in Howe's nineteen games tells its own story. Only a large stroke of luck on the last day of the season kept City afloat; while they withered to defeat at Villa Park, already-relegated Notts County beat Luton to secure City's place in the following season's inaugural Premier League.

Bobby Gould (1992–3)

Gould returned to take up the managerial reins nearly 10 years after his first attempt and opinions on him were divided. Within a week of the season starting, City had won three out of three and sat top of the newly formed Premier League; the blistering start continued with six wins out of eight matches, and a memorable season seemed to be taking shape.

That early season promise had just started to fade by the autumn, until, with his eye for a bargain very much intact, Gould snapped up the portly figure of Mick Quinn. The number nine's job was simply to finish the chances the team had been creating and he did just that – scoring 17 league goals in little over half a season. Quinn's incisiveness in the penalty area complemented the speed and trickery provided by Gallagher, Williams and Ndlovu, to give the Sky Blues attack a genuine cutting edge.

Five-goal shows over Liverpool and Blackburn were highlights as the Sky Blues cemented a place in the top eight for most of the season, and the outlook was bright. A disappointing late slump of one win in eleven, coinciding with the sale of Robert Rosario, saw the Sky Blues slide down to a final fifteenth place. Despite the late drop down the table, Gould's return was a definite success; his attack-minded team had often thrilled the fans and hopes were high for his second season.

The Sky Blues began the following year with a fantastic 3–0 win at Arsenal, courtesy of a Quinn hat-trick and were unbeaten in their first eight games. Gould seemingly had a solid base to build on, but within a month he had resigned, citing pressure to sell star striker Ndlovu. It was a disappointing exit for a hometown manager who loved the club and was generally succeeding.

Phil Neal (1993–5)
After a 5–1 thrashing at QPR, Bobby Gould immediately resigned leaving his assistant Phil Neal in charge. Neal had enjoyed a stellar club career at Liverpool and had already solidly managed Bolton Wanderers, so he had much experience to offer. His shrewdness was quickly apparent as he engineered a very respectable eleventh-place finish; though his resources were not fantastic, Neal

seemed to know what to do with them and in particular, Ndlovu and Babb blossomed.

Neal's second season began dreadfully with just two points taken out of the first fifteen, including two 4–0 reverses. The manager did not panic though and his answer was inspired. Manchester United striker Dion Dublin was struggling to get games at Old Trafford and was hungry for first-team opportunities which the Sky Blues could offer. Dublin arrived for a hefty £2 million and began in blistering fashion with eight league goals in his first ten starts. At last, City had a genuine target man, a goal-threat and a leader on the pitch. Despite Dublin's terrific impetus, the Sky Blues continued to struggle and a run of twelve games without a win sealed Neal's fate. This was possibly harsh on Neal, who could cite the perennial City bosses' lines of limited resources and always having to sell off your best players (this time Phil Babb to Liverpool). But harsh or not, a higher-profile City was about to emerge.

Ron Atkinson (1995–6)

When Ron Atkinson arrived at Highfield Road he was every bit the archetypal modern football manager; much-travelled and much quoted, suntanned and successful. With 'Big Ron' at the helm, City were suddenly guaranteed to make the headlines.

For Atkinson's first home match an extra 5,000 supporters arrived and their high hopes were rewarded with a convincing win against West Ham. The team progressed nicely for a time, boosted by new signings Kevin Richardson and million-pound defender David Burrows, and relegation fears seemed unlikely, until a dip in form at Easter. A late-season win at Spurs, inspired by the veteran assistant manager Gordon Strachan, saw City ease to safety.

After a busy summer period in which Big Ron boosted his squad with three more million-pound signings – Telfer, Salako and Williams – 1995/96 promised much. With money being spent and Atkinson's ability to talk a good game, many supporters believed that the years of struggle were to become a thing of the past. However, the season didn't work out that way. Promising early signs were soon forgotten as the team went fourteen games without a win, before then strangely thrashing champions Blackburn 5–0 in the snow. Atkinson's answer to the team's poor form was simply to buy more and more players: before Christmas it was Richard Shaw and Noel Whelan; after Christmas it was Liam Daish and Eoin Jess – with transfer fees ranging from £1 million to £2 million, none were cheap.

The huge influx of cash did not correspond with a huge increase in points and the Sky Blues again left it to the final game to secure their Premiership status. Once safety was assured though, Atkinson talked about going places in 1996/97, but despite yet another major signing, this time Gary McAllister from Leeds, the team could not get out of the bottom three. It turned out that the only place Atkinson was heading for was the mythical 'upstairs' (football club speak for anywhere apart from near the first team), to become a newly created Director of Football. Although he occasionally contributed to the City cause from a distance, it was Big Ron's soundbites, rather than his sound footballing decisions, that lingered in the memory.

Gordon Strachan (1996–2001)
Gordon Strachan arrived as Atkinson's assistant in March 1995 and the long-term plan was for him to succeed his more experienced boss in a couple of seasons. Barely 18 months later, however, Strachan took over the

manager's role after Atkinson's reign had stalled. It was a position he held for close to 5 years; that length of time alone was testament to his success.

Strachan's first, fire-fighting season ended in a glorious relegation escape. An unlikely combination of results allowed the Sky Blues' final-day win at Tottenham to be decisive and from there Strachan's team made solid progress. The 1997/98 season saw the Dublin and Huckerby partnership blossom; combining both pace and nous, the duo were the Sky Blues' best striking pair for a generation. An agonising FA Cup quarter-final exit in a penalty shoot-out to Sheffield United was the year's low point, while winning seven consecutive games was the highlight.

The following year saw the departure of Dion Dublin and, subsequently Strachan's team struggled, finishing a disappointing fifteenth. Unusually though, the board showed patience and support for Strachan and they backed their man with the exciting buys of Moroccan duo Youssef Chippo and Mustapha Hadji. Although the Sky Blues only climbed one place in the league table by the end of the 1999/2000 season, the Sky Blues had delivered some outstanding home performances that year which thrilled their fans.

Strachan lost several experienced players that summer – McAllister, Whelan, Keane – and it showed immediately as his final full year turned into a desperate fight to avoid relegation. Unlike previous seasons, this team simply could not score enough goals, or win enough games, and when the death knell was sounded on City's 34-year stay in football's elite, few fans were surprised. The bigger surprise was probably that Strachan stayed on in a bid to take the club straight back up; his seasons of relative success had clearly gained him credit in the eyes of the City board. Within a handful of games of the new season though it was clear that Strachan had finally run out of credit with the fans; large-scale protests greeted a dismal home defeat to Grimsby and the 'Wee Man' was gone; his mostly solid record was inevitably soured by a relegation which left a very bitter taste.

DID YOU KNOW?

Boy Wonder
One of the stars of England's number one-ranked cricket team (at the time of writing), Ian Bell, has Sky Blue connections. As a schoolboy, Bell showed ability at football as well as cricket, and in the 1990s he spent time honing his footballing skills at the Sky Blues School of Excellence – despite actually supporting Aston Villa!

When Bell left football behind, City's loss became Warwickshire and then England's gain, as the Coventry-born batsman has gone on to enjoy a spectacular cricket career. Three Ashes victories, sixteen Test match centuries and a reputation for being one of the most stylish batsmen in the world today suggest Bell made the right move in swapping goal nets for cricket nets!

Are You Watching Jimmy Greaves?
An unusual chant followed City on their way to Wembley in 1987 – the refrain 'Are you watching Jimmy Greaves?', gathered momentum as the cup run gathered pace.

The cheery ditty first emerged when City played away at Old Trafford in the fourth round. TV pundit and ex-England goal-grabber Jimmy Greaves opted for a United win, only for City to prevail thanks to a Keith Houchen toe-poke. Undeterred, Greaves then went on to tip City's opponents in each of the following rounds. As each prediction unravelled, City fans latched onto the fun of proving the pundit wrong and the chant 'Are you watching Jimmy Greaves?' emerged.

By the time they reached the final at Wembley, Greaves' predictions had almost become a part of City's pre-match preparation. Greaves, of course, was a big pal of his ex-Chelsea team-mate, John Sillett, who was to lead the Sky Blues to their proudest day, and the suspicion lurks that he took great pleasure in City's triumph, despite his own Tottenham connections.

The Little Big Man

When John Sillett signed Chelsea's David Speedie in the summer of 1987, he was adding plenty of qualities to the cup-winning team. Speedie was a highly rated Scottish international striker, very much at the peak of his powers, and securing his services was a real coup for City.

Speedie brought with him many impressive attributes: a terrific touch, an eye for goal and, for a man only 5ft 7in tall, an unbelievable heading ability. Although he only saw red twice in nearly four years in Sky Blue, Speedie also brought with him a fiery, competitive nature and short fuse which meant trouble – with referees or centre-backs – was often on the horizon. While opposing fans loved to taunt him, Speedie remained a firm favourite with the City faithful, who were treated to some moments of the highest quality. Exquisitely chipped goals became one of the Scot's trademarks, with efforts at Norwich and QPR standing out from a high-class collection.

For a small man, his heading ability was almost freakish; his determination and timing in the air meant he regularly outjumped players much taller and stronger than him. Perhaps at his best in the autumn of 1988, Speedie twice managed the remarkable feat of scoring a hat-trick of headers at Highfield Road. He was a striker to savour; a bundle of trouble with a bag full of tricks.

THE FOUNTAINS WERE BLUE!

16 May 1987 was the day when unfashionable, underachieving Coventry City defied predictions to win the FA Cup. For Sky Blue fans everywhere, their unlikeliest dreams came true. The final was popular outside of Coventry too and is still regarded as one of the finest in living memory. The match had just about everything; it became a see-saw encounter with five goals; there was a spectacular strike, as good as any ever scored at Wembley, and it was the archetypal David v Goliath FA Cup fare.

When Brian Kilcline hobbled up the steps to collect the famous old trophy, the thousands in the stadium and the many more watching in their living rooms at home were united in joy, the likes of which the city of Coventry has seldom seen. Within moments of Kilcline raising the cup aloft, the ghostly, empty roads in the city seemed to fill up with motorists blaring their car horns in a chorus of celebration.

The signal had been given and it was to be a weekend of extraordinary happiness. As the city centre filled up, fans danced, drank and even kissed their way though the night; the revellers revelled and the onlookers cheered them on; Sky Blue scarves adorned Godiva's statue and the city centre fountains were dyed sky blue! It was like a hundred New Year's Eves had been rolled into one glorious, uproarious night.

When the team paraded the cup on an open-topped bus the next day, a sea of people, estimated at some 250,000, filled the streets and bobbed alongside the crawling bus. From grandmothers to newborns, and just about every age in between, almost everyone was out applauding their Sky Blue heroes; a city simply smiled.

Other titles published by The History Press

Coventry Then & Now
978-07524-5994-3
The historic city of Coventry has a rich heritage, which is uniquely reflected in this fascinating new compilation. Contrasting a selection of eighty archive images alongside full-colour modern photographs, this unique book captures how the city used to be and how it looks today.

Coventry's Motorcycle Heritage
978-07509-5125-8
Considering Coventry was the birthplace of the British cycle industry, it is perhaps no surprise that the city became heavily involved in the development of the British motor industry during the mid-1890s. From the first velocipedes built here in 1868, most of the later well-established cycle manufacturers quickly turned their attention to motorised vehicles, and many of the early motoring pioneers moved to Coventry to become part of this revolutionary work.

Visit our website and discover thousands of other History Press books.

www.thehistorypress.co.uk